AN A–Z ADVENTURE

THROUGH THE

PLANT KINGDOM

Christina Harrison

Lauren Gardiner

Kew Publishing
Royal Botanic Gardens, Kew

First published in 2016 by the Royal Botanic Gardens,
Kew, Richmond, Surrey, TW9 3AB, UK
www.kew.org

ISBN 978 1 84246 614 8

Distributed on behalf of the Royal Botanic Gardens, Kew in North America by the University of Chicago Press, 1427 East 60th St, Chicago, IL 60637, USA.

British Library Cataloguing in Publication Data
A catalogue record for this book is available from the British Library.

Production Management: Andrew Illes
Illustrations: Livi Mills
Layout: Nicola Thompson, Culver Design
Cover design: Livi Mills

Print Managed by Jellyfish Print Solutions.

For information or to purchase all Kew titles please visit shop.kew.org/kewbooksonline or email publishing@kew.org

Kew's mission is to be the global resource in plant and fungal knowledge, and the world's leading botanic garden.

Kew receives about half of its running costs from Government through the Department for Environment, Food and Rural Affairs (Defra). All other funding needed to support Kew's vital work comes from members, foundations, donors and commercial activities, including book sales.

Contents

PREFACE

Plants are amazing. They are also weird, wonderful, ugly, beautiful, 'clever', enormous, tiny, poisonous, and life-saving. As we both work at the Royal Botanic Gardens, Kew, it probably goes without saying that we are fascinated by plants, but we are also excited by how many unusual and fantastic new plant stories we hear all the time – from bizarre uses of plants to discoveries of strange new interactions between plants and animals, insects or fungi. Not to mention just how many completely new plant species are still being discovered and described (around 2,000 every year).

We've filled this A–Z adventure through the plant kingdom with as many diverse and interesting stories as we could fit in. We could have added so many more, but we hope this selection whets your appetite and makes you curious to find out more. Our aim has been to bring you the message that plants are astonishing, and ultimately that we all depend upon them. Their diversity is the fundamental basis of life on Earth. Unfortunately many plant species are threatened with extinction worldwide. It's time to celebrate and marvel at the plants around us: they are part of our history, our everyday lives and our futures, and they deserve our whole-hearted admiration.

CHRISTINA HARRISON AND LAUREN GARDINER

ACKNOWLEDGEMENTS

We would like to thank our colleagues at Kew for their encouragement, their stories and their help, especially Mark Nesbitt, the publishing team and Kew's library staff.

We would also like to acknowledge the following for their story ideas and help:

Colin Clubbe	Daniel Hourigan	Katie Price
Rhina Duque-Thues	Andrew Jackson	Thomas Walton
Carolyn Fry	Tony Kirkham	Richard Wilford
Serene Hargreaves	Heather Lindon	Emma Williams
Ruth Harker	Stephanie Pain	Gail Vines

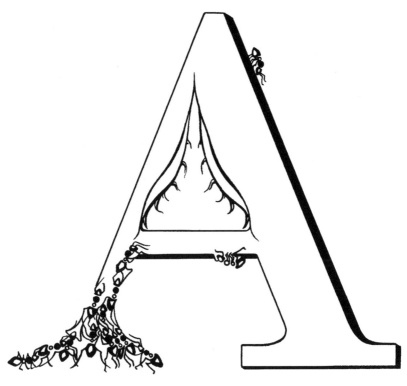

is for...

Alcoholic Agave

How often do you think that the century plant (*Agave americana*) flowers? If you said 'every hundred years' you'd be way off. The name is completely misleading as this species usually flowers every 20–30 years, but it is very slow growing. Once it has built up enough energy reserves, this large spiny succulent sends up a flower spike that can reach a dizzying nine metres in height. Unfortunately, this plant is monocarpic – meaning that once it has flowered and set seed, it then dies.

Agaves are full of sugary sap – several species are harvested purely for their 'agave nectar', which is used as an alternative to sugar. This has also been put to use for centuries in the production of tequila – where the sap from *Agave tequilana* is fermented, distilled and turned into the well-known alcoholic drink.

Alzheimer-Fighting Bulbs

Snowdrops and daffodils are always a welcome sight in spring, reminding us of new beginnings and the vibrancy of life. They can be especially cheering when you're not feeling well or are unsure of the future.

However, these bulbs can do more than simply raise the spirits of those people suffering from mild vascular dementia or Alzheimer's disease. Some species of snowdrop (*Galanthus*) and daffodil (*Narcissus*), as well as other bulbs including snowflakes (*Leucojum*), contain galantamine, which has been shown to help nerve cells in the brain communicate with each other, thereby relieving some symptoms.

Originally solely produced from harvests of these species (including *Galanthus woronowii*), the licensed medication – under the name Reminyl – is now also produced synthetically to cope with demand. This is a perfect example of how plants can contain the medications we desperately need, and why their conservation is important.

ANGRAECUM ASSOCIATIONS

These stunning star-shaped orchids from Madagascar come complete with long flower spurs filled with sweet nectar. The spurs are specialised structures that allow only certain species of moth to reach the nectar inside.

Charles Darwin famously studied the comet orchid (*Angraecum sesquipedale*) and predicted that only a moth with a proboscis 35 cm (over 13.5 in) long could possibly access the nectar and, in doing so, pollinate the flower. No such moth was known to exist at the time, and his theory was held in doubt and even ridiculed. Over twenty years after Darwin's death, a moth (*Xanthopan morganii praedicta*) with a proboscis exactly the right length was discovered and the great naturalist was proven right.

More recently, in 2008, a PhD student called Claire Micheneau began studying *Angraecum* species on the island of Réunion, to see how they were adapted to pollinators there. What was pollinating *Angraecum cadetii* was a particular mystery. Claire knew that pollination was taking place, but hours of observation revealed no clues. Rigging up a motion-sensitive night camera, she caught a completely unknown species of raspy cricket (since named *Glomeremus orchidophilus*) in the act. To find a new species, and to find it doing something completely unexpected, was a revelation. Further evidence that the cricket was the true pollinator of the orchid was found in that the cricket's head was exactly the right size to fit inside the opening of the nectar spur.

As the moths that usually pollinate *Angraecum* species in Madagascar were not present on Réunion, new alliances must have been formed. Claire also found that two other species of *Angraecum* were being pollinated by white-eye songbirds, but the cricket remained the big surprise, using its long antennae to locate the flower in pitch darkness. This was the first time a cricket had been recorded as an orchid pollinator.

Botany Hero

Agnes Arber (1879–1960)

A renowned plant morphologist and anatomist, Agnes Arber had a remarkable impact on botany and botanists. She attained a first class degree from University College London and then headed to Cambridge University, where she worked for over 50 years. She published eight books (now considered classic texts) and over 90 scientific papers, which she also usually illustrated herself. She was the first female botanist to be elected as a Fellow of the Royal Society in 1946 (on the same day as 24 men). She was also the first woman to be awarded the Gold Medal by the Linnean Society (their highest award for contributions to science), in 1948.

Arber was considered by her peers to be the most distinguished plant morphologist of her time. Her work focused on monocotyledonous plants – plants that germinate with one initial seed leaf, such as grasses, bulbs and palms. She was also interested in, and published on, the history of botany, and the philosophy of biological research and thinking. Interestingly, because Cambridge University did not award full degrees to women until 1948, Arber could not take out books from the University Library unless a man signed for them.

Ants in your Plants

Ants are always on the look out for a meal, and plants are always coming up with ingenious ways to get insects to do their bidding. Many species of plant offer ants an incentive to carry their seeds away and plant them underground by way of a fat-rich attachment on their seeds called an elaiosome. The ants carry the seeds back to their nests and feed the elaiosome to their larvae, discarding the seed. The seed benefits from being hidden away out of the reach of predators, droughts and fires, and is also perfectly placed to germinate when spring comes.

When ants disperse a plant's seeds it is known as myrmecochory (sometimes spelled myrmechory). This is common in dry habitats such as the fynbos of South Africa, dry woodlands of Australia, and habitats across the world with a Mediterranean climate. However, you can see this in action much nearer to home, as many of us grow an elaiosome plant in our gardens – the dainty cyclamen.

Astonishing Atacama

Seeing the Atacama Desert in bloom must be the holy grail of the botanical world. The desert is enormous, running approximately 1,000 km (over 600 miles) from northern Chile to the south of Peru, with the Pacific Ocean to the west and the Andean mountains separating the desert from the rest of the South American continent to the east. One of the driest places on Earth, some parts of the desert have not experienced a drop of rain since records began, and only the North and South Poles are considered to be drier.

The barren lunar – or rather Martian – landscape has been used to test Mars rovers. Yet in spite of the extreme climate and the apparent absence of life, the flora of the desert is rich and diverse, with approximately 1,000 native vascular plant species. More than half of these are 'endemic', which means they are only found there and nowhere else.

Plants in the Atacama Desert are adapted to the extremely dry conditions and their seeds can survive in what is known as the 'soil seed bank' for many years, waiting for the right conditions to trigger germination, as often happens in El Niño years. In March 2015, heavy rains hit the southern part of the desert and 're-awoke' seeds in the soil. Seeds across an enormous area germinated at the same time, and by September many thousands of young plants were flowering en masse, including rare species of *Nolana* (Chilean bell flower), creating vast colourful carpets of wildflowers in yellows, oranges, pinks and purples, as far as the eye could see. A stunning and breathtaking natural phenomenon.

ATOMIC-BOMB-PROOF

Ginkgo biloba is sometimes described as a 'living fossil'. What we know as an elegant street tree today is actually an extremely old evolutionary branch of the plant kingdom – one that grew at the same time as when the dinosaurs roamed the planet during the Jurassic period. Its common name is the maidenhair tree, but its Latin name is thought to be derived from the Japanese name 'gin kyo', meaning 'silver apricot'.

Not only has this species lasted millions of years relatively unchanged since it evolved into the form we see today, but *Ginkgo* seems to be extraordinarily resistant to forces that would kill most other plants – from severe weather through to the blast of an atomic bomb.

Six *Gingko* trees grow just 1–2 km (around a mile) from the centre of Hiroshima, Japan, having survived the 1945 bombing. At that distance from ground zero, virtually everything else living died instantly, but the burnt trees survived, re-grew and are still growing today. These six trees, along with other plants that survived the nuclear blast – from weeping willows to fig trees – are called *Hibakujumoku* in Japanese, meaning 'survivor trees'.

Azolla

One of the fastest-growing plants in the world, *Azolla* is a tiny freshwater fern (sometimes called duckweed fern) that can multiply at an astonishing rate. It is proving to be highly invasive in our rivers and waterways, sometimes completely choking them. Unlike many other plants *Azolla* can take nitrogen directly from the atmosphere owing to symbiotic cyanobacteria (*Anabaena*) in its leaves. This ability allows the plant to double its biomass every few days.

But this little plant's highly invasive nature is not a new thing – around 50 million years ago its seasonal blooms covered the entire North Pole, greening the Arctic Ocean (then an enclosed body of water). Its vast extent and fast-growing abilities were to play a key role in climate history. Back then, summer temperatures could reach 25°C (77°F) at the North Pole, and atmospheric carbon dioxide (CO_2) was around six to seven times higher than today.

Azolla plants sequestered enormous amounts of CO_2 inside their cells, which sunk with them to the sea floor once they died. It is estimated that this species drew down around half of the CO_2 in the atmosphere at that time, cooling the planet and changing the world completely. This discovery was made in 2004 and has become known as 'The Azolla Event'.

Scientists are researching whether this plant could provide an alternative to expensive climate-regulating technologies, with research on its genome hopefully providing the answers to its runaway ability to reproduce.

is for...

Buoyant Balsa

One of the lightest woods in the world, balsa comes from the fast-growing South American tree *Ochroma pyramidale*. When alive, balsa timber is spongy and full of large water-filled cells. Once kiln-dried, however, the empty cells mean that the wood is not only extremely light, but also considered the strongest wood for its weight in the world.

Much of the world's commercial crop of balsa comes from Ecuador, and it is put to many uses including insulation, fishing floats and buoys, as well as crafts such as modelling. It was even used in full-sized Second World War aeroplanes and, famously, for the raft on the 1947 Kon-Tiki expedition by Thor Heyerdahl. Balsa is the Spanish word for 'raft'.

Banksia

Banksias are weird yet wonderful looking plants. Their fat flower-heads are made up of hundreds of tiny flowers and look like sturdy bottle-brushes. They come in a variety of bright colours, appealing to a range of pollinators who come to devour the plentiful nectar the plants produce. There are over 170 species of *Banksia*, all but one of which are endemic to Australia, where they grow in mainly arid landscapes.

An interesting variety of animals visit *Banksia* flowers, including birds, bats, rodents and even possums. Some species are pollinated by honey possums – a tiny marsupial whose long slender snout and tongue are perfectly adapted for getting nectar from the long, narrow flowers.

Banksias are highly adapted plants. Some species can withstand fires by hiding part of their stem underground. This 'lignotuber' can withstand heat and the plant can regrow from it, but most rely on the tenacity of their seeds to survive. Their bizarre-looking fruits or 'follicles', which develop from the flowers, are woody cone-like structures with closed mouth-like apertures along their surface. In most species the follicles sit tight on the plant or on the ground and only open after the heat of a bushfire. The ash-covered ground forms a perfect seedbed, with no other plants to shade the new seedlings or compete for resources.

Did you know? The genus name, *Banksia*, honours the English botanist, de facto first director of the Royal Botanic Gardens, Kew, and President of the Royal Society, Sir Joseph Banks. Banks first collected specimens of three species of these plants in 1770 at Botany Bay, when he accompanied Captain Cook on the HMS *Endeavour* expedition. They were some of the first plants he gathered.

BEZOARS (AND BANANAS!)

Be careful eating wild bananas on your tropical travels. The 17 million cultivated bananas grown and sold today are almost all the 'Cavendish' cultivar of *Musa acuminata*. Around the world though, many people eat wild bananas, relatives of the cultivated varieties, which have not had some of their more unpleasant features removed by selective breeding.

The fruits of all bananas contain tannins, which give the fruit an astringent taste when they are unripe. As cultivated bananas ripen, the tannins are inactivated and they lose their astringent taste. This doesn't seem to happen in wild bananas, and when eaten the tannins can interact with pectins (from plant cell walls) and other compounds to form insoluble complexes.

When combined with the large number of hard seeds found in wild bananas (selectively bred out of cultivated varieties), rock-like masses called 'bezoars' can form in the stomach and gut, which can cause serious gastric problems including potentially life-threatening bowel obstructions. These are thought to account for an alarming number of deaths in tropical areas of the world with poor medical care, where such obstructions all too often cannot be diagnosed or treated in time.

Did you know? If the word 'bezoar' sounds familiar, you might remember it from J. K. Rowling's books about a young wizard. In *Harry Potter and the Philosopher's Stone*, during Professor Snape's potion lessons the first year student wizards are taught that these stone-like masses 'from the stomach of a goat' can be used as an antidote to most poisons, including the venom of the Basilisk. In *Harry Potter and the Half-Blood Prince*, Harry saves Ron's life with a bezoar after Ron drinks poisoned mead meant for Professor Dumbledore.

Biodiverse Brazil and her Beautiful Nuts

Brazil is the most biodiverse country on Earth, home to more than 46,000 species of plants and fungi, of which just over 19,500 grow nowhere else on the planet. Six major types of ecosystems or 'biomes' exist, namely Amazon tropical rainforest, Atlantic tropical forest, dry woodland known as Caatinga, lowland plains called Pampas, savannah, and a vast wetland called the Pantanal.

There are over 2,500 species of orchids, hundreds of palm species, towering hardwood trees, and many valuable crops including the brazil nut tree (*Bertholletia excelsa*). Brazil is named after the leguminous tree known locally as 'pau brasil' (*Caesalpinia echinata*), an important source of timber.

Brazil nut trees are at the centre of a complex ecological web of organisms that depend on each other's existence to survive. Removing one species from this web could ultimately cause the extinction of the others. The brazil nut tree depends on species of euglossine bees to pollinate the flowers. It also depends on a large forest rodent called the agouti, which has strong enough teeth to crack open the hard, woody fruits and disperse the seeds so that they will germinate and grow into new trees. The pollinating bees depend on the flowers of a particular species of orchid, *Coryanthes vasquezii*, from which the male bees collect scented wax, which they use to attract the females in order to mate.

Because the production of brazil nuts depends on this natural web they are difficult to farm agriculturally; unfortunately sustainable harvesting of brazil nuts is also proving problematic too. A number of scientific papers have shown that brazil nut trees are not regenerating properly in forests because so many fruits containing the nuts are harvested. To replace trees that die as they age, more fruits need to be left to germinate naturally, to produce young trees.

BISON GRASS

You know a plant is either useful or deadly when it has many common names. Bison grass is also commonly known as sweet grass, but also peace grass, Mary's grass, unity grass and vanilla grass, among many other names. Its Latin name *Hierochloe odorata* derives from the Greek for 'holy fragrant grass'.

This hardy plant is found growing across northern Europe and North America and has been put to use wherever it grows, mainly because of its sweet vanilla-like aroma. The scent is released when the leaves are crushed and is due to the chemical coumarin – one of the compounds responsible for the fragrance produced by pods of the vanilla orchid. Coumarin is often used in perfumes, but it is also used to manufacture the anticoagulant drug warfarin.

The leaves of bison grass grow horizontally along the ground, reaching up to 100 cm (39 inches) long, and were once harvested for strewing on floors, especially in European churches on Saints' days. They were also gathered by basket weavers, and were used for flavouring sweets, tobacco, tea, and, perhaps most famously, vodka. You'll still find a single blade of bison grass in every bottle of the Polish vodka Żubrówka.

In North America, bison grass has been used traditionally as a medicine for colds, as an analgesic, and as an insecticide. The grass was also soaked in water and then used as an infusion to wash in. Carl Linnaeus (see **L, Botany Hero: Carl Linnaeus**), considered the 'Father of Taxonomy', reported that bison grass was sold in Sweden to hang over beds to induce sleep. Overall, a pretty useful plant to have around.

Boojum Tree

One of the weirdest looking 'trees' you'll ever see, this plant's common name is said to come from Lewis Carroll's poem *The Hunting of the Snark*:

> *But if ever I meet with a Boojum, that day,*
> *In a moment (of this I am sure),*
> *I shall softly and suddenly vanish away ——*
> *And the notion I cannot endure!*

The boojum (*Fouquieria columnaris*) is found in only two places in the world – Baja California and a small part of Sonora, Mexico, where strange-looking plants seem to abound. To continue the literary theme, the boojum tree also looks like something straight out of Dr Seuss – its thin tapering trunk grows straight upwards and then sometimes completely curls over. It is covered in short spiny twigs with tiny deciduous leaves, while its main branches stick out at odd angles.

Some have described this plant as looking like an upside-down carrot. It is more accurately known as a 'stem succulent', and its swollen trunk retains water for the plant to use in times of drought. The spines deter hungry and thirsty animals from taking a juicy mouthful.

BOTANY HERO
HARRIET MARGARET LOUISA BOLUS
(1877–1970)

The most prolific female botanist ever, in terms of the number of new species described and published, was the South African Harriet Margaret Louisa Bolus. Great-niece of the influential botanist and philanthropist Harry Bolus, she published 1,494 new plant species during the course of her career.

After studying teaching and completing a Bachelor degree in literature and philosophy, Harriet Bolus worked as an assistant to her great-uncle at the herbarium he had founded at the University of Cape Town in 1865. When Harry passed away in 1911, a condition of his substantial bequest to the University was Harriet's continued employment as the curator of what is now the oldest functioning herbarium in South Africa.

Harriet went on to become a founding member of the Botanical Society of Southern Africa, and over her career she wrote a number of textbooks and many research papers, becoming one of South Africa's most prolific and influential botanists, all in spite of having no formal scientific training.

BRIGHTEST BLUE

The most intense blue in nature is found in the fruits of the marble berry, *Pollia condensata*, from Africa. This dazzling spectacle is not generated by a pigment, but rather by the structure of the surface of the fruit. Layers of coiled microfibrils in the cells of the super-smooth fruit wall selectively interfere with incoming light to reflect only the brightest metallic blue. A similar effect is seen in the wings of *Morpho* butterflies and the feathers of some birds including kingfishers.

Burs and Barbs

The age-old problem for plants of how to disperse their seeds and produce the next generation, has been solved in myriad ways. Many plants around the world have evolved brightly coloured, juicy, and/or fragrant fruits, enticing animals and birds to dine on them and take the seeds away to be deposited within a useful dollop of nutritious dung.

Some plants can eject their own seeds using elaborate mechanisms (see **F is for Far-Flinging Seeds**), while others just let the wind carry their seeds away to (hopefully) germinate wherever they might land.

Another clever dispersal mechanism comes in the form of burs – seed capsules with an elaborate range of hooks, teeth and barbs that catch onto passing animals and people's clothing. Some, such as cleavers (*Galium aparine*) and cockleburs (*Xanthium strumarium*) are relatively harmless, but others can cause injuries, including the grapple plant (*Harpagophytum*) from South Africa and *Tribulus terrestris*, which goes by various wickedly inventive common names including puncture vine and devil's thorn.

One of the most impressive-looking burs grows on a genus of plants known as devil's claws (*Proboscidea*) from North America. These alien-looking seed pods are some of the largest botanical hitchhikers in the world. Each has two large curved woody hooks, like horns, which clasp onto the fur or legs of passing animals. It is thought that they may have evolved when much larger animals roamed the landscape, before the last Ice Age.

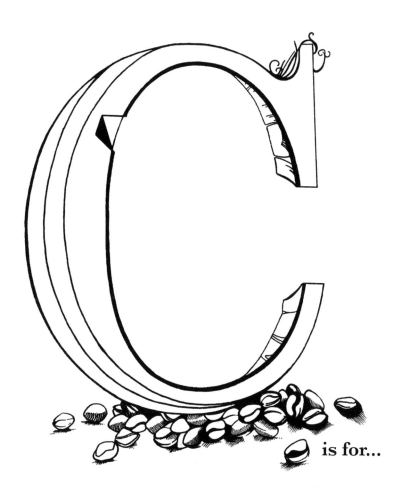

is for...

Caffeine Buzz

Plants have an extraordinary arsenal of tricks at their disposal in order to attract pollinators and keep them coming back – including bright petals, UV honey guides (see **U is for Ultraviolet Signposts**), pollen, scent and of course nectar. Plants compete with each other daily for these visitors and readily bribe them in order to get the job of pollination done.

However, it's been found recently that some species have another trick up their sleeves – adding a dash of caffeine to their nectar. This isn't about pepping up pollinators, it's about memory. Caffeine helps honeybees to remember the flower as a good source of nectar – it helps create loyalty and keeps them coming back, meaning other flowers of the same species are more likely to be pollinated.

That coffee species do this is perhaps no surprise, but it's been found that citrus species do it too. In fact, 13 other genera of plants have been found to produce caffeine in their nectar, for possibly the same reason. The scientists who discovered this, from Newcastle University and the Royal Botanic Gardens, Kew, believe that this may not just have an effect on honeybees, but other bees and insects too. As part of the UK Insect Pollinators Initiative, they are continuing to study the effects of natural chemicals in nectar and how this influences pollinator behaviour.

CHLOROPHYLL CHEMISTRY

Chlorophyll is perhaps the world's most important compound, powering the planet by converting pure sunlight into energy inside plant cells. Chlorophyll is the green pigment found within the chloroplast structures inside leaves. It uses blue and red wavelengths of light to initiate the series of chemical reactions required to turn CO_2 and water into carbohydrates and oxygen – the process known as photosynthesis. The green colour of chlorophyll, and therefore most leaves, is due to the fact that it absorbs much of the red and blue wavelengths of light that hit it.

CHROMOSOMES

The double-helix strands of DNA in the nucleus of every living cell are tightly wound into structures called chromosomes. It might be logical to assume that the more complex an organism, the more genes it needs to function, and so to conclude that more DNA (and of chromosomes) would be found in each cell. However, research has consistently disproved this theory.

The amount of DNA in a single copy of a cell's genetic material is called the genome size, and flowering plants contain the widest variation in genome size in nature. The smallest genome, that of the carnivorous plant *Genlisea aurea*, is just 64 megabases (Mb) of DNA, but the Japanese canopy plant, *Paris japonica*, has 2,400-times that amount in each of its cells, amounting to 149,000 Mb of DNA. If all of this DNA was uncoiled from the chromosomes, the total length would be longer than 12 London buses placed end to end, all from one single plant cell!

Coconuts could Save your Life!

Desert island cartoons always include a solitary coconut tree (*Cocos nucifera*), hanging over the beach, with the shipwrecked traveller sitting below, looking forlornly out to sea. That innocuous, handsome coconut tree could easily save the traveller's life.

Coconut water is enjoying a surge in popularity as a healthy beverage and even as an electrolyte-rich 'superfood'. Health claims aside, the water inside a coconut has long been a staple part of tropical diets, being refreshing and good for replacing lost fluids and salts from the body after sweating.

In places with poor sanitation and unreliable drinking water sources, coconut water is often one of the few safe drinks to consume – although be warned, the fluid can act as a diuretic, and drinking the contents of a full coconut is not to be recommended before a long car or bus journey. If you cut yourself and need to wash the wound, cracking open a coconut and using its water as a sterile rinse is a much better idea than using potentially dirty tap- or seawater.

Interestingly, it is possible to overdose on coconut water. Its high level of potassium, and also calcium and magnesium, make it particularly unsuitable for those with kidney failure or severe burns. In 2014, a medical journal reported an otherwise healthy man who drank 2.5 litres (0.6 US gallons) of coconut water during one day, as a sports drink for fluid replacement, being admitted to hospital after fainting. He was found to have an unusually slow heart rate and blood pressure, signs of kidney and muscle damage, and a life-threateningly high level of potassium in his blood. All these symptoms were later attributed by doctors to his consumption of coconut water.

Did you know? Coconut water forms naturally inside the developing coconut. Coconut milk is made from grated coconut flesh, which is blended or soaked in water, squeezed and then sieved.

CO-EVOLUTION

Since flowering plants first appeared during the Cretaceous Period (around 100 million years ago) they have continued to evolve. Over time, many plant species have co-evolved alongside the insects, mammals and birds that act as their pollinators and seed dispersers. Some plant species have become so specialised that, in some cases, only one species of insect can now access their nectar, and so pollinate them (see **A is for Angraecum Associations**).

Some neo-tropical passionflowers (*Passiflora*) have been locked in an ongoing co-evolution battle with longwing (Heliconiinae) butterflies for thousands of years. The butterflies pollinate the flowers, but they also like to lay their eggs exclusively on passionflower leaves. The larvae have voracious appetites so this is a major problem for the plant. The passionflowers evolved to produce a poison in their leaves as a chemical defence, but instead of putting the caterpillars off, the caterpillars evolved to be able to store these chemicals and use them in their own defence against their predators.

The passionflowers also evolved to produce different leaf shapes to fool the butterflies from laying their eggs on them. Particularly impressive however are those species of passionflower that have evolved leaves with yellow spots, or blobs, at the base of their leaves, to make it look as if they already have eggs on them and so deter the butterflies from laying their own.

The evolution of passionflower species and their butterfly pollinators is a classic case of co-evolution – both species are dependent on each other and both are continually evolving specific traits to increase their own chance of survival, but with neither ever getting the upper hand.

CORK OAKS

Cork is one of the most sustainable and renewable natural resources in the world. It is made from the bark of the cork oak tree (*Quercus suber*), native to south-west Europe and north-west Africa. The bark of the tree is harvested by being stripped away in sections by hand, exposing an orange-red layer underneath. It is then left to grow again in a nine-year cycle of harvesting.

Cork is the periderm, the outer layer of tree bark. Its unusual structure resembles a honeycomb, and is over 50 per cent air. The tissue contains high levels of suberin – a waxy substance that is highly hydrophobic (water repelling). Owing to its elasticity, low density, insulating and lightweight properties, cork is used to make an astonishing variety of products including flooring, insulation and acoustic tiles, shuttlecocks, fishing floats and wine bottle stoppers, all of which are biodegradable.

Each cork tree can live for up to 200 years and be stripped of its bark around 15 times if the harvesting is performed properly. In their native range, cork oak forests cover nearly 30,000 km² (over 11,500 square miles). Roughly a third of this is in Portugal, which produces around half of the world's cork harvest. It is thought that the insulating properties of the thick bark may have evolved to protect the tree from forest fires.

The cork forests in Spain and Portugal in particular are home to a wide variety of wildlife, including the endangered Iberian lynx. Sustainable harvesting of cork forests supports local economies as well as protecting these biodiverse and increasingly rare habitats.

CRYPTIC CRYPTOGAMS

Cryptogams are an intriguing collection of species that reproduce using spores rather than seeds. They include algae, lichens, mosses, liverworts and hornworts, ferns and horsetails, as well as fungi. Together they make up an enormous proportion of the world's botanical diversity.

The name 'cryptogam' comes from the Greek *kryptos*, meaning hidden, and *gameein*, meaning to marry, referring to their mode of reproduction (once considered mysterious), which produces no seeds.

What is thought to be the world's first site of special scientific interest (SSSI) for cryptogams was created at Wakehurst Place in Sussex. Named the Francis Rose Reserve in 2010, this site is 25 hectares (62 acres) in size and is carefully managed to conserve these lower plants and fungi, including rare species such as the Tunbridge filmy fern (*Hymenophyllum tunbrigense*).

is for...

Danger, Don't Touch!

We tend to think that only animals have the ability to bite us, thanks to their often sharp teeth made of a number of minerals including calcium phosphate. Recently, however, researchers at the University of Bonn have discovered this mineral in the stinging hairs, or trichomes, of some members of the rock nettle family (Loasaceae) in South America.

The mineral provides immense strength to these stinging hairs, maximising their defence against a wide range of hungry herbivores. Any browsing animal foolish enough to try to eat one of these plants would soon regret it – if the tips of the hairs are broken off, they deliver a rush of inflammatory chemicals that leave sensitive mouths and tongues in considerable pain.

Our common stinging nettles (*Urtica dioica*) only strengthen their stinging hairs with glass-like silica, although that's still enough to get our attention.

BOTANY HERO
CHARLES DARWIN (1809–1882)

A few years after Darwin returned from his travels around the world he settled down with his wife, Emma Wedgwood (of the pottery dynasty), and began a family. Ever the logical scientist, weighing up the options, Darwin had previously made a list of the pros and cons of getting married.

The pro-marriage column included:
- children (if it please God)
- constant companion (and friend in old age) who will feel interested in one
- object to be beloved and played with – better than a dog anyhow
- home and someone to take care of house
- charms of music and female chit-chat ... these things good for one's health

Darwin's reasons against getting married included:
- freedom to go where one liked
- conversation of clever men at clubs
- not forced to visit relatives and bend in every trifle
- to have the expense of children
- loss of time – cannot read in the evenings
- fatness and idleness
- less money for books etc.

Darwin spent his last forty years living at Down House, Kent, where he maintained an extraordinary level of correspondence with colleagues, friends and acquaintances around the world – writing more than 7,500 letters – alongside writing his many important scientific papers and books. These included *On the Origins of Species* and *On the various contrivances by which*

British and foreign orchids are fertilised by insects, and on the good effects of intercrossing. So much for not having time once married!

Introducing their theories of evolution, and what would come to be known as natural selection, the joint paper *On the Tendency of Species to form Varieties; and on the Perpetuation of Varieties and Species by Natural Means of Selection* by Charles Darwin and Alfred Russel Wallace was read at the Linnean Society of London in 1858. Contrary to popular belief however, the initial reading of the paper and its subsequent publication, containing their most famous and influential theories, didn't cause much of a stir. The President of the Society, Thomas Bell, later said in his summing up of 1858: 'The year which has passed … has not, indeed, been marked by any of those striking discoveries which at once revolutionize, so to speak, the department of science on which they bear.'

DAWN REDWOOD

One of the greatest botanical finds of the first half of the 20th century, the dawn redwood (*Metasequoia glyptostroboides*) was originally thought to be extinct, as it was only known from the fossil record of 1.5 million years ago. It was only recognised by palaeobotanists as a genus in its own right in 1941. However, in the same year as it was being named as a relic, a forester came across an enormous and unusual tree, which locals called a water fir, in the forests of China. By

1946 Chinese botanists had made the connection between the two and the dawn redwood became a celebrity as a 'living fossil' – a plant risen from the realms of ancient extinction.

The dawn redwood is very similar in appearance to the swamp cypress (*Taxodium distichum*) and is related to the coastal redwood (*Sequoia sempervirens*) and the giant sequoia (*Sequoiadendron giganteum*). This tall, elegant, coniferous tree is deciduous like the swamp cypress – its soft needle-like leaves turn reddish-brown before falling in autumn. It grows in open forests, prefers moist areas near rivers and is usually found in valleys.

Although seeds of the dawn redwood were widely distributed to arboreta around the temperate world to help with its conservation and many are now planted as ornamental trees, it remains endangered in the wild. It has been protected by Chinese law since 1980 but populations are highly fragmented within intensively used landscapes, and its future remains uncertain.

DRACULA DECEPTION

Mimicry in plants is absolutely fascinating. In particular, the range of things that plants have evolved to mimic in order to attract pollinators is truly astonishing. One such example is the *Dracula* orchids that grow in the cloud forests of Ecuador. These plants lure in fruit flies as pollinators by pretending to be mushrooms. Despite being commonly known as fruit flies, most Drosophilid flies seek out fungi on which to feed and breed.

Dracula orchids have evolved a specialised petal (called a labellum) that bears a remarkable visual and tactile resemblance to a mushroom. They also emit a mushroomy scent, which completes the allure, and tricks the flies into pollinating them.

Did you know? *Dracula* orchids derive their name from the original translation of the Latin name 'little dragon', rather than coming from the novel by Bram Stoker. Having said that, in 1978 the US botanist Carlyle Luer published a species called *Dracula vampira*, playing on both the literary association and also the rather sinister look of the black, stripy, angular flower.

DRAGON'S BLOOD

On an isolated island in the Indian Ocean you'll find a weird-looking tree that oozes ruby-red sap from its bark. This remarkable species has been prized since ancient times, and the blood-like resin has been used for both medicine and magic. This is the dragon's blood tree (*Dracaena cinnabari*).

This slow-growing evergreen tree is endemic to the semi-tropical island of Socotra, off the coast of Yemen. Its symmetrical tightly-packed umbrella-like canopy gives the tree an odd appearance, but this helps it to survive arid conditions. Water is efficiently channelled down from its waxy leaves towards its roots, and the canopy provides a dense shade, to reduce water loss.

The red resin oozes from fissures or wounds in the bark to help protect the tree from infection. However, people have long harvested the resin to use it as a dye and varnish to colour and decorate their houses and goods (as well as themselves). It also has a history of being used in a variety of traditional medicines.

Although this unique tree and its woodlands are protected, the species is under threat from human activity and climate change.. A third of the plant life on Socotra is endemic, occurring nowhere else on Earth. Many of the species are so unique that the island has been described as 'otherworldly' and 'the most alien-looking place on the planet'.

is for...

Eat your Reds (and your Greens)

Anthocyanins are truly extraordinary. These natural red, blue and purple flavonoid pigments are not only found in flowers and fruits, giving them vivid enticing colours, but in leaves, stems and roots too. Anthocyanins are responsible for much of the blaze of autumn colour we enjoy in a wide range of plants. They are actively produced in leaves towards the end of summer as the sugars and chlorophyll pigments are broken down. The results can be spectacular – as seen in New England in the United States. The autumn colours of the forests there are so vivid they can even be seen from space.

But that is not the only extraordinary thing about anthocyanins. Plants rich in these pigments, such as bilberries, raspberries, blackcurrants, red cabbage and some grapes, among many others, can be extremely beneficial to our health. Anthocyanins are thought to interact with other phytochemicals to produce antioxidant and antimicrobial effects, be beneficial for vision disorders, reduce cancer cell proliferation and control cardiovascular disease. They may also help prevent obesity and diabetes.

Anthocyanins have also been credited with helping to enhance memory. How they may do all of these things is not fully known, but one thing is for sure – as well as eating your greens, you should also be eating your reds and purples.

ECHO-LOCATION

When you're relying on bats to find you at night, you might as well make yourself as obvious as possible to them. One Caribbean rainforest vine species, *Marcgravia evenia*, has come up with an ingenious way to ensure it is visited by these nocturnal nectar-loving visitors.

This plant has unusual concave dish-shaped leaves on top of its inflorescences, which reflect echo-locating clicks back to a bat over a wide angle. Scientists at the University of Ulm in Germany found that this helped bats to find the plant in half the time it would otherwise, ensuring that the spectacular blooms are located and pollinated.

EGYPTIAN EMBALMING

Among the many beautiful and extraordinary things discovered in and around the ancient tomb of Tutankhamun were a host of botanical remains. There were jars of resins, oils, perfumes and incense, perhaps including frankincense (*Boswellia*) and myrrh (*Commiphora myrrha*). Food, drink, and other botanical offerings were left in baskets for the Pharaoh's journey into the afterlife. Scientists at the Royal Botanic Gardens, Kew helped to identify some of the plant remains from the tomb, including timbers, seeds and flowers.

It is often the mummy and the art of embalming that really fascinates people. The Greek historian Herodotus claims that once the body had been emptied of its organs, it was 'cleansed with palm wine' (from the date palm, *Phoenix*), although no direct evidence has been found to substantiate this. Others have suggested that scented oils and spices such as cassia may have been used in mummification, but unfortunately, after all this time, little hard evidence exists for that either.

In his book *Pharaoh's Flowers*, Kew scientist Nigel Hepper describes how Tutankhamun is thought to have been embalmed in the traditional way – washed and oiled, and then wrapped in layers of linen bandages (made from the flax plant, *Linum usitatissimum*) among which were placed juniper berries (*Juniperus communis*).

Once the body was mummified, fresh floral garlands or collars, sewn onto a base of papyrus (*Cyperus papyrus*), were draped over the body, and also left elsewhere in the tomb. Even after 3,000 years the elements of these garlands and bouquets are still recognisable. They include olive and date palm leaves, pomegranate and willow leaves, wild celery, blue lotus petals, cornflowers and chamomile, as well as *Withania* berries. The body was then anointed with fragranced oil before being sealed away.

ELEPHANT GRASS

Elephant grass (*Pennisetum purpureum*) is one of the most useful grasses to have around in its native Africa. Although it can be an invasive species, this robust tall perennial has been put to use by farmers as a living fence and windbreak around their crops. It is also a crop in itself, as the young shoots make good hay for dairy cows and it can be cut for fuel too. Elephant grass can grow in relatively dry conditions and helps to both improve soil fertility and prevent soil erosion. But this is not the end of its virtues for the farmer.

This species is being used in a 'push and pull' agricultural system developed by scientists in Kenya and the UK, which aims to prevent crop damage by stem-boring insects. It is difficult to attack these insects with insecticides (which are also expensive), so this system uses both a repellent and an attractive plant to deter the pests. The repellent plant is grown among the crop to push the pests out, while the other – such as certain varieties of elephant grass – is planted around the edge to lure the insects out of the crop to lay their eggs on them instead.

If implemented properly this strategy is highly effective, reducing pests by around 50 per cent and increasing yields significantly – which means more secure food supplies for thousands of people.

ENCEPHALARTOS

This genus of primitive-looking cycads includes some extremely rare species. Native to Africa, *Encephalartos* species have been around since the time of the dinosaurs, but today some species only exist in small wild populations. One of them, Wood's cycad (*Encephalartos woodii*), can claim to be possibly the rarest plant in the world as it only exists in the wild as a single specimen in South Africa.

As cycad plants are either male or female, and one of each is needed to produce a new generation, no new specimens of this species can ever be grown from seed. Thankfully, cycads produce vegetative offsets also known as 'pups' at their base, and some of these have been grown on in botanic gardens. A specimen of the remarkable *E. woodii* can be seen growing at the Royal Botanic Gardens, Kew.

Did you know? The name *Encephalartos* is based on the Greek for 'bread in the head'. The pith of the cycad's stem is toxic, but by scraping it out and burying it for two months, the toxins are broken down and the tissue can be kneaded and then baked into a bread.

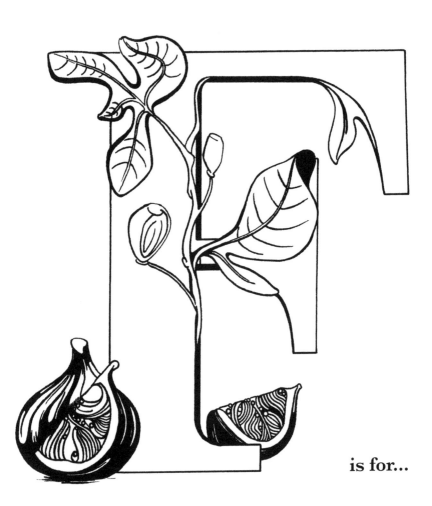

is for...

Famous Names

It might not come as a surprise to know that there is a wide range of organisms named after British broadcaster, naturalist and all-round national treasure, Sir David Attenborough. From the botanical world alone there is a Welsh member of the daisy family called *Hieracium attenboroughianum*, a critically endangered pitcher plant from the Philippines called *Nepenthes attenboroughii*, and a single-species genus in the Annonaceae family (the family containing custard-apples and soursops) called *Sirdavidia*.

It might be more surprising to know that there are two begonias named after characters from *Star Wars* – *Begonia darthvaderiana* and *Begonia amidalae*, an orchid named after *Sesame Street's* Oscar the Grouch called *Stelis oscargrouchii*, and another named for the dragon in J. R. R. Tolkien's book *The Hobbit* called *Dracula smaug*. There is also a genus of ferns named *Gaga* after the pop singer Lady Gaga. In 2016, a newly-described species of tomato from Australia, *Solanum watneyi*, was named for the botanist character Mark Watney, played by Matt Damon in the movie *The Martian*.

The botanists who name species and genera must follow a precise set of naming rules when they publish new discoveries and classifications, using a code called the 'International Code of Nomenclature for algae, fungi and plants'. Although a rigorous and strict set of rules, the Code does not place many restrictions on what, where or who taxa can be named for – although others might scoff, you really can name the new species you've discovered after your pet, your favourite footballer, or your partner. Do note though, although there's technically no rule against doing so, it's considered the ultimate bad form to name a taxon after yourself.

FAR-FLINGING SEEDS

Plants have evolved some ingenious ways to disperse their seeds as far away from themselves as they can, so avoiding competition for space, light and nutrition with their offspring. The sandbox tree (*Hura crepitans*), native to tropical America, must hold a record for the distance it can catapult its seed – hurling it up to 45 metres (147 ft) through the forest, at an average speed of 43 metres per second (or over 150 km per hour/ 90 miles per hour). Its fruits literally explode to release the seeds, earning it another of its common names – the dynamite tree.

FASTEST FLOWER

You may not think of flowers as moving quickly in any way, especially when they belong to a plant called the creeping dogwood (*Cornus canadensis*). However, this small woodland plant is pretty extraordinary in this regard. In late spring, it produces tiny white flowers (2 mm across) with highly 'elastic' petals. These can flip open in an astonishing 0.2 milliseconds, releasing the pollen-bearing stamens with a force that is 2,400 times that of gravity and thereby launching pollen into the air.

While the pollen is only ejected 2.5 cm (0.07 in) above the flower, this is an impressive ten times the height of the flower and easily allows the pollen to be picked up the breeze and carried away to pollinate other flowers. Insects can trigger the flowers to spring open, and the pollen hurtles upwards to stick to their body hairs, allowing the pollen to then be carried to another flower. The opening of the creeping dogwood flower is one of the fastest plant actions so far recorded.

BOTANY HERO

LEONARDO FIBONACCI (C.1170–C.1250)

Plants produce some beautiful, artistic, and often mathematically interesting, patterns. One of the most well-known geometric patterns, seen in many plants, including the spiral of a pine cone and the arrangement of sunflower seeds in a seed head, is the Fibonacci sequence.

The sequence starts off 0, 1, 1, 2, 3, 5, 8, 13, 21 ... , with each number being the sum of the two numbers before it. The man who popularised the sequence is usually referred to as Leonardo Fibonacci, but this wasn't his name at all. Born in Pisa, Italy, in the 12th century, Fibonacci was actually called Leonardo Pisano (literally 'Leonardo of Pisa'). It was not until Pisano's handwritten copies of his works were being transcribed by scholars hundreds of years after his death, that the words 'filius Bonacci', meaning 'son of Bonaccio', on the title pages were misinterpreted as being Pisano's name – and the name 'Leonardo Fibonacci' was born.

To explain the Fibonacci sequence, Pisano used the example of how quickly rabbits could breed. If a pair of rabbits produced one pair of rabbits as offspring, that pair would reach sexual maturity at one month old and could then produce another pair themselves after a month's gestation, and so forth. Each month the number of pairs of rabbits would be equal to the sum of the number of pairs of rabbits in the previous two months. After 12 months, assuming throughout that no rabbits die, there would be 233 rabbits – the 14th number in the Fibonacci sequence.

From breeding patterns to honeybees, Nautilus shells to the arrangement of leaves on a plant stem, the Fibonacci sequence is seen repeatedly in nature. Why and how evolution has converged on this pattern so often is not fully understood, but in the case of seed heads and leaves on stems, it has been shown that these Fibonacci arrangements provide the optimal and most efficient number of seeds or leaves for the area available.

Fish Poison Tree

Sometimes the common names of plants relate exactly to the use they are put to, and this species is a great example. The fish poison tree (*Barringtonia asiatica*), from Asia and the Pacific Islands, contains the poison saponin, which is particularly concentrated in its seeds. Traditionally, the angular fruits and their seeds are pounded to a pulp to help release the poison, and then thrown into streams to stun fish.

As with many 'poisonous' plants, it is the dosage which makes a plant chemical helpful or harmful. In low doses, the seeds and leaves of this tree are used as a traditional medicine – for treating coughs and lung problems, stomach- and head-aches, as well as for worms and other parasites.

This tree is also appreciated for its beauty. It can be seen planted as a shade tree near the coast in its native regions, particularly in Singapore, where its beautiful, fragrant, pompom-like flowers are greatly admired.

Fruity Figs

Who has ever seen a fig flower? You probably know what the fruits look like – bulbous and purple-green with a small hole at one end. Not so many people know that when you cut a fig in half, the individual thread-like structures you see are what remains of the fig's flowers, hidden from view, inside.

Some fig (*Ficus*) species produce separate male and female inflorescences (structures on which the flowers are borne) whereas other species produce figs that have a male phase and a female phase. In both types, the flowers are hidden inside a swollen structure called a synconium. When the flowers inside a female synconium are pollinated, the fertilised ovaries swell, resulting in an enlarged, juicy, sweet fig filled with numerous small seeds.

The only way that the pollen from the male fig flowers can get to the female flowers is via a mutualistic relationship with fig wasps, which have co-evolved with the plants. The female fig wasp crawls inside a fig via the small hole at the end. As she moves around inside she will pollinate female flowers with the pollen she has carried from the male fig that she hatched inside. She lays her eggs, which develop and eventually hatch, and the young wasps burrow their way through the fig's tissues before emerging into the outside world. The female wasp dies inside the fig, and the tissues around her release enzymes to digest her body and absorb what is left.

FRUITS NOT VEGETABLES

Did you know that a cucumber is a fruit and not a vegetable? The best clue is that a cucumber has seeds inside – which a vegetable does not. Other fruits commonly labelled as vegetables include butternut squash, olives and aubergines, as well as pea pods, courgettes, peppers and tomatoes.

Fruits are the seed-bearing parts of a flowering plant produced when the flowers have been pollinated, while vegetables are non-reproductive, vegetative parts of a plant such as leaves, stems or roots and tubers. Vegetables include cabbage, lettuce, beetroot, broccoli, celery, rhubarb, potatoes, onions and many more. So, technically, next time you have a salad, it may be that you're eating a fruit salad ...

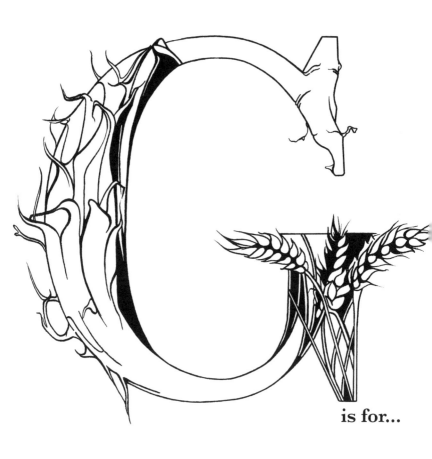

is for...

Geophytic Ground-Huggers

Geophytes are plants that have the ability to retreat underground when conditions become unfavourable – be that due to frost and cold, or even heat and fire. You'll be familiar with a whole range of geophytes as many of them are bulbs. Geophyte literally means 'ground plant', and the term includes any type of plant that can die back to an underground storage organ – bulb, corm, tuber or rhizome – and then regrow when conditions are more suitable.

The underground part of the plant contains food reserves that help it to regrow quickly. Geophytes are found throughout the world, but the strategy is a real advantage to those that need to survive droughts, and for those that need to grow rapidly and compete for resources. Many are found in areas with a Mediterranean climate, including the Cape region of South Africa, and particularly in the Karoo – a semi-desert region.

In the Karoo, several geophyte genera have adopted unusual growth forms to help them survive – including having their leaves lying flat to the ground, or growing extremely curly leaves. *Massonia* species have two large flat succulent leaves, between which a pompom-like flower emerges. The species *Massonia depressa* produces a highly viscous nectar that attracts rodents such as gerbils, which act as its pollinators.

Did you know? *Massonia* was named after Francis Masson, the first official plant hunter for the Royal Botanic Gardens, Kew, in the 18th century (see **O is for Oldest Pot Plant in the World**). He travelled the Cape and collected over 500 species during a period of twelve years.

Botany Hero

Lilian Suzette Gibbs (1870–1925)

A well-travelled botanist, full of character and ideals, Lilian Gibbs was an inspiration. Born in London, Gibbs trained in botany at the Royal College of Science (now Imperial College) and was a passionate plant collector and field naturalist, becoming an expert in montane plants, as well as working and publishing on 'lower' plants such as mosses and liverworts.

She travelled widely in Europe, Africa, Iceland, Fiji, New Guinea, New Zealand, Australia and Tasmania, among other places, plant collecting wherever she went. She was the first European woman and the first botanist to climb Mount Kinabalu in Borneo in 1910, where she collected new species and contributed many botanical specimens for the British Museum. She was particularly interested in the geographical distribution of plants.

In 1910 she was awarded the Huxley Medal and Prize for research by Imperial College. She was one of the first women to be elected to the Linnean Society (1905) and the Royal Microscopical Society (1910), and joined the Royal Geographical Society in 1919. The plant genus *Gibbsia* was named after her, and several species bear her name, including the New Zealand moss species *Calobryum gibbsiae*, the conifer *Podocarpus gibbsiae* and the bamboo *Racemobambos gibbsiae*, commonly known as Miss Gibbs' bamboo, both from Mt Kinabalu.

Gibbs died in Tenerife in 1925 aged just 54, and is buried there. Today this kind of travel and work may seem simply admirable for the career of a female botanist, but in the context of the time she was living Lilian Gibbs achieved an astonishing amount and was a truly remarkable botanist.

GLUTINOUS GRASSES

An often much maligned part of our diets nowadays, gluten is the component of wheat flour that gives bread its characteristic springy, elastic texture. As anyone who has to, or chooses to, eat a gluten-free diet knows, finding gluten-free bread that does not crumble and is able to replicate this soft, chewy texture is a rare treat.

Only produced by some members of the grass family (Poaceae), gluten is a specific combination of proteins (mostly gliadin and glutenin) found in their seeds' endosperm. When the embryo of a seed germinates, the endosperm provides the nutrients for the embryo to grow, until the young seedling is able to obtain its own nutrition via its new leaves and roots. Most plant seeds have an endosperm (see **T is for Tiniest Seeds in the World** for some seeds which don't), but different groups of plants have different components making up the endosperm of their seeds.

When bread dough is kneaded, the gluten proteins gradually turn into a network of elastic fibres that trap the CO_2 being produced by the yeast included in the mix. The more the dough is kneaded, the longer the fibres and the more elastic the network produced. The amount of kneading therefore changes the 'rise' of the loaf, produced as the CO_2 inflates the dough, and the resulting texture of the cooked bread.

But not all grasses contain gluten. In spite of its name, glutinous rice (found across Asia in an amazing range of savoury and sweet dishes) is naturally gluten-free, as are all rice species and cultivars. Also known as sticky rice, glutinous rice is so-called because of its sticky texture when cooked, a result of high levels of the starch amylopectin in its endosperm – nothing to do with gluten at all.

GROWING WITH GRAVITY

Have you wondered how plant stems 'know' to grow upwards towards light, and how roots 'know' to grow downwards into the earth? This is particularly noticeable when germination occurs, but even if fully grown plants are knocked over, stems can re-orientate their direction of growth, or new shoots can begin to grow in a vertical direction in a relatively short space of time.

The great scientist Charles Darwin pondered this question too. Put simply, he said gravity dictates to the plant the direction in which it should grow. Darwin observed how the cells in the very tips of the roots were essential for roots to grow downwards into the soil.

Since his work, much more research has been done on gravity 'receptors' in plants. These receptors, called 'amyoplasts', occur inside specialist cells in the root cap and tip, and contain starch grains that are like pebbles in a tumbler. If the root is moved sideways, away from the direction of gravitational pull, then the grains tumble towards the new 'bottom' of the cell. This accumulation, working in conjunction with plant hormones called auxins, then determines the new downwards direction for growth.

In plant stems, the detection of gravity by specialist cells occurs all along the stem, and not only allows straight vertical growth in primary stems, but also helps plants to position their leaves in the best orientation to gain maximum light for photosynthesis. New research is looking at how the external structure of each plant cell also plays an important part in detecting the position of a cell in relation to gravity.

Knowing how plants detect gravity can assist agricultural plant breeders in producing the most productive forms of crop plants. It is also helping scientists to understand how plants react to micro-gravity in space (see **Z is for Zero Gravity**).

GRUESOME

The identification of plants and plant parts can be remarkably informative to archaeologists and forensic investigators. Plants can provide vital clues about the time and place of events – as many only grow in particular areas and tend to flower or fruit at specific times.

One gruesome case that required specialist plant knowledge was passed to scientists at the Royal Botanic Gardens, Kew in 2001. A headless torso had been found floating in the River Thames near Tower Bridge. Pathologists and investigators knew it was a young boy, and thought he had been trafficked to the UK and ritually sacrificed. Beyond establishing the fact that he was Nigerian, investigators were unable to identify the victim, and he became known as Adam.

The Forensic Science Service sent images of Adam's stomach contents to Kew's scientists, who determined that calabar beans had been ground down and given to the boy to sedate him. Further work also revealed the presence of *Datura* – a powerfully toxic plant (see **Z is for Zombies**) – in Adam's stomach. Although some progress has been made on the Adam case, he has still not been officially identified and no-one has been charged with his murder.

Calabar beans come from the climbing leguminous plant *Physostigma venenosum*, which is poisonous to humans if chewed or ground up into food. The beans are the seeds of the plant, and contain alkaloids, including physostigmine, which affect the nervous system and brain. Native to south-east Nigeria, the plant has been recorded in ritual ceremonies. In the past, it was 'ordeal poison' given to determine the guilt or innocence of people accused of witchcraft. If you survived being forced to eat the beans, you were innocent. If you did not, you were guilty, and died painfully and slowly from the toxins in the beans.

is for...

HADES FLOWER

It's not really surprising that a plant that has no leaves, grows underground, and 'drains the goodness from the roots of trees and shrubs' has come by the name of the Hades flower. Known scientifically as *Dactylanthus taylorii*, this 'unseen one, presiding over the underworld' is New Zealand's only fully parasitic plant.

The only two ways to spot this threatened plant are by the 'wood roses' it creates – flower-like patterns that form on the swollen root of the plant off which it is feeding, and by its own flowers. Towards the end of summer, the Hades flower sends up numerous inflorescences of around 50 very simple musk-scented flowers, each laden with nectar to attract pollinators. Unfortunately, nearly all of its natural pollinators have disappeared. The plant's only known pollinator, the endemic lesser short-tailed bat, is increasingly endangered.

However, recent studies of 800-year-old mummified poo from the rare flightless nocturnal parrot known as the kakapo, have revealed that it also once had a taste for Hades nectar. Conservationists are now trying to put these two unusual species back in the same habitat where both can be fully protected. In 2012, eight birds were released on Little Barrier Island in the north of the country – a haven for native species – in the hope that they may ensure the future of this little plant of the dark realm.

HALLUCINOGENIC

More than a few plants are used by people for the hallucinogenic effects they induce. One of the most famous is the peyote cactus (*Lophophora williamsii*), which is native to Mexico and southern Texas, where it is found in arid limestone scrublands. The peyote is a squat little spineless cactus containing mescaline which the cactus produces as a form of defence instead of having sharp spines. Mescaline is a strong hallucinogen that leads to a change in visual perception, hallucinations, and what is referred to as an altered state of consciousness. In Britain mescaline powder is classified as a Class A drug.

The peyote cactus has been used by Native American peoples for thousands of years – both for rituals and for medicine – and certain tribes continue this use today in religious ceremonies. The effects of peyote last for between 10 and 12 hours, but they are not without their negative side effects – including vomiting, diarrhoea, panic and anxiety.

Illegal collecting of peyote by recreational users, and land-use change in its native range, are reducing the numbers of this psychedelic little plant, and it is now classed by the International Union for Conservation of Nature (IUCN) as being 'Vulnerable' to extinction.

HEAVIEST PLANT IN THE WORLD

The Trembling Giant in Fishlake National Forest, Utah, USA, is a colony of quaking aspens (*Populus tremuloides*). The colony is viewed by some as being biologically one individual, as each tree is a clone, and it is therefore said to be both the largest living organism on Earth and the heaviest – weighing in at an estimated 6,000 tonnes (over 6,600 US tons).

The clonal colony covers 43 hectares (over 100 acres) with around 45,000 trunks, which are all genetically identical and connected by one root system underground. Its age is difficult to determine because the stems are always being replaced, new ones growing and old ones dying.

Some people think the colony may be 80,000 years old, others say it's much older, however each tree may only be 100 years old so 'age' here is a very relative concept. The colony has also been nicknamed 'Pando' – Latin for 'I spread'.

Quaking aspens often form clonal stands. They are beautiful trees with smooth white bark and heart-shaped leaves that flutter in the breeze – a habit that has inspired both their common and Latin names.

HIGH LIFE

We're all familiar with the sight of moss and lichen growing on tree trunks, but have you ever stopped to think about how they survive without obvious roots, simply sitting on the tree?

They are examples of epiphytes, sometimes known as 'air plants'. Epiphytes grow (mostly) harmlessly on other plants and get their nutrients from the air and rain, unlike parasitic plants such as mistletoe, which draw nutrients from the host on which they are growing. Some epiphytes, such as bromeliads, also collect debris in and around them to help produce a nutrient-rich soil-like humus, which helps to support them (see **T is for Tanks up Trees**).

Many different types of plant have adopted this mode of living, especially in tropical forests where it helps them to grab a better spot, away from herbivores and other plants competing for space, nutrients and light. Mosses, lichens, liverworts and ferns, as well as many orchids and bromeliads, and even some cacti, are epiphytic, . Some do grow roots, but usually only to attach to their host plant or to help them absorb water.

Epiphytes add a whole new layer to forest ecosystems and have a wide range of relationships with the insects and animals that live there.

BOTANY HEROES

WILLIAM JACKSON HOOKER AND JOSEPH DALTON HOOKER
(1785–1865 AND 1817–1911)

Father and son William and Joseph Hooker not only created the modern foundations of the Royal Botanic Gardens, Kew, but also made a significant impact on botanical science as we know it today.

Sir William Jackson Hooker was Regius Professor of Botany at Glasgow University, and became the first official director of Kew in 1841. During his directorship, he greatly expanded the Gardens, and oversaw the building of the Palm House and Temperate House – two of the greatest Victorian glasshouses ever built. He also started the Gardens' Herbarium and Economic Botany Collection.

His son Joseph Dalton Hooker was both an adventurer and a pioneer of modern science. He travelled with Captain Ross in 1839 to survey the Antarctic, and spent three years collecting plants in the Himalayas, where he caused an international incident when accused of trespassing, and was held prisoner by the Raja of Sikkim. On his travels he collected an astonishing 7,000 species in India and Nepal, including 31 species of *Rhododendron*, 25 of which were new to science.

Joseph Hooker forged the way for gentlemen to become 'professional' scientists – being paid for their endeavours while also remaining respectable – a new idea at the time. He not only wanted to document plants, but to understand why they grew where they did, and he became a great friend of Charles Darwin, encouraging him to develop and publish his theories. One of Joseph's legacies was to devise an important and influential plant classification system with another botany great, George Bentham, which became the standard system worldwide until the late 20th century and the introduction of a DNA-based classification system. Joseph became director of Kew after his father retired and was also the first professional botanist to become president of the Royal Society.

Hot, Hot, Hot!

In recent years, chilli growers have been vying with each other to create the hottest chilli on record. One called 'Red Savina' held the top spot with a Scoville Heat Units (SHU) rating of 577,000, until the 'Bhut Jolokia' broke the 1 million SHU mark, followed by the 'Naga Viper' and 'Trinidad Scorpion' – names not to be trifled with.

In 2013, the 'Carolina Reaper' registered a scorching 1,569,300 SHU and became the current *Guinness World Record* holder. It is claimed that it has also been measured at 2,200,000 SHU. When you consider that your average jalapeño is somewhere between 2,500 and 5,000 SHU, you get some sense of how mind-blowing the heat of this spicy vegetable must be. Ethnobotanist James Wong has estimated that a single 'Carolina Reaper' could be used to make 500 litres (over 130 US gallons) of curry!

The heat in a chilli pepper (the fruit of certain *Capsicum* species) is due to chemicals known as capsaicinoids, which are concentrated in the membrane surrounding the seeds inside the fruit. The concentration of these chemicals varies between varieties, but also between plants depending on their growth conditions. When eaten by humans, these natural chemicals trigger a rush of endorphins, which can induce a sense of euphoria, and it is this that some people start to crave.

The 'heat' in chillies is measured in Scoville Heat Units, named after Wilbur Scoville, who developed a measurement test in 1912. An extract of the chilli is diluted in alcohol to extract the capsaicinoids, and then diluted in a solution of sugar water. This is then tasted and further diluted until the heat becomes undetectable – the more dilution required, the hotter the chilli.

Did you know? Only mammals are affected by a chilli's heat – chilli fruits have evolved to be consumed by birds which, completely unaffected by their heat, disperse the seeds in their droppings.

BOTANY HERO
ALEXANDER VON HUMBOLDT
(1769–1859)

More things are named after Alexander von
Humboldt than anyone else. These include
places, flora and fauna, an ocean current and
even an area on the Moon. Humboldt was an
extraordinary man and explorer, as well as a
great thinker and scientist. In the words of his
biographer Andrea Wulf, he simply 'wanted to
know and understand everything'.

Born in Germany to a wealthy family,
Humboldt was adventurous from an early age.
He loved nature, preferring to spend his time
exploring and collecting. Between 1799 and 1804
he travelled the Americas, with the authorisation
of the King of Spain, and was often one of the
first westerners to visit and describe areas, plants,
animals and native peoples. He explored the
Orinoco River in Venezuela and discovered its
link to the Amazon. He also travelled in Cuba, the
Andes and Mexico. In the United States he met
and impressed President Thomas Jefferson. Later,
he completed a major expedition through Russia.

Humboldt worked in an astonishing variety
of disciplines – studying and making major
contributions to cartography, geography, biology,
climatology and geology, and devised theories
on the Earth's magnetism. He developed a new
approach to natural science – combining all the
major disciplines in order to understand the

bigger picture, finding connections everywhere. He believed in nature working as a living whole or 'web', as demonstrated by his *Naturgemälde* drawing showing how habitats and species changed with altitude and temperature.

One of Humboldt's greatest skills was in communication. He wrote many books on his travels and theories that were popular with the public. He also inspired many other scientists including Charles Darwin (see **D, Botany Hero: Charles Darwin**). Almost 300 plant species are named after him including Humboldt's lily (*Lilium humboldtii*), the orchid *Phragmipedium humboldtii,* as well as species of oak, cactus, bladderwort, geranium and a willow.

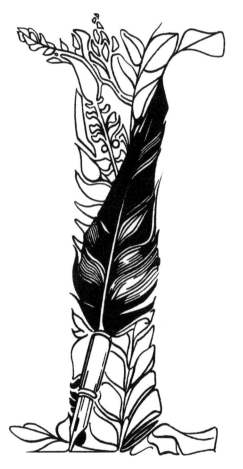

is for...

INDIGESTIBLE PAPER

Edgeworthia chrysantha is a beautiful winter-flowering fragrant shrub. It can be seen in many gardens and is native to hillsides and forests in southern China and the eastern Himalayas. It is related to another well-known winter-flowering and highly fragranced shrub – *Daphne.*

Edgeworthia is also known as the oriental paper bush as its bark is used to create quality handmade paper – including the highly valued mitsumata paper in Japan. Japanese bank notes used to be made from *Edgeworthia,* and were considered to be the hardest notes to forge.

In Sikkim, legal and government documents that need to be archived have long been printed on paper made from *Edgeworthia,* due to its strength, flexibility and natural antifungal and anti-pest properties. Documents made of *Edgeworthia* paper do not rot or go mouldy, and insects tend to ignore them.

INTERNATIONAL RESCUE

In 2010, a tiny packet of minute fern spores was carefully collected on the isolated Ascension Island, in the South Atlantic, and airlifted to the UK in a daring effort of international rescue. The spores were delivered to scientists at Kew for them to attempt to grow the critically endangered fern *Anogramma ascensionis* and save it as a species.

The fern, known as the Ascension Island parsley fern, had been thought to be extinct after it hadn't been seen for some

50 years, but after four plants were found on a cliff edge in 2009, the race was on to secure the fern's survival.

Using a paintbrush, Kew's scientists transferred the spores to a nutrient agar jelly and incubated them in a light room in sterile conditions until they germinated. The experiment was successful, and in 2013 and 2014 small fern individuals were repatriated to Ascension Island and grown on in the island's nursery. Once large enough, a number of ferns were planted out into the wild, near to the original four plants. Less than six months later, the new plants were found to be growing well and had started to produce spores themselves.

Iron Gall Ink

For hundreds of years, until the end of the 19th century, writing ink was commonly made from oak galls. These strange round growths can be found protruding from the leaf buds of oak trees (*Quercus* spp.) and are caused by the larvae of gall wasps.

To make ink, people harvested the galls and fermented them to extract the tannin or gallic acid. This was then added to iron sulphate, gum arabic and water to make a permanent ink that darkens gradually as it is exposed to air. There was a real art to making this ink properly as it was easy to get the proportions of ingredients wrong. Natural dyes could also be added to create different coloured inks. Iron gall ink was particularly used on vellum; when used on paper the acidity of the ink sometimes caused problems, although many old documents survive in perfect condition today.

Some of the earliest recipes for iron gall ink are almost 2,000 years old, and it was widely used during the Middle Ages. Many of our most important documents, books, music scores, letters and drawings were made using it. These odd little marble-like galls have helped us to record our history.

(Vegetable) Ivory

Ivory was all the rage in Victorian society, long before anyone was particularly concerned about the ethics and implications of elephant hunting. But ivory was expensive and difficult to procure, so the search for alternative materials that could retain the same look and feel like real ivory became big business.

The fruits of a number of so-called vegetable ivory palms (including the most commonly used, the Ecuadorean species *Phytelephas aequatorialis*) – are big, spiky and quite ugly, but hold a treasure inside. The hard white endosperm of the four or more large egg-shaped seeds inside the fruit makes an excellent substitute for animal ivory. Each is, on average, 5 cm (almost 2 in) long, and the material can be carved, polished and dyed different colours, and is strong and relatively dense. The most prized of these 'tagua nuts' or 'ivory nuts' are not only large, but also have no cavity or markings, so they produce pure white pieces with no blemishes.

By the late 1800s the trade in tagua was enormous, and by the start of the 20th century it was worth US $5 million. Vegetable ivory was used to make a wide range of items including buttons, chess pieces, cutlery handles, dice and billiard balls. In the 1920s, 20 per cent of all buttons produced in the US were made of vegetable ivory. However, the Second World War and the invention of new synthetic materials like plastic polymers meant that the trade in vegetable ivory from South America had collapsed by the 1950s.

Nowadays, tagua is still used to make jewellery, buttons and small carved artefacts, mostly for tourists and as artisanal exports from South America. Increasingly tagua is being marketed as a sustainable non-timber forest product that supports local economies and enables local people to protect threatened natural forests.

is for...

Jade Vine

One of the most beautiful and striking of all tropical climbing plants, the jade vine (*Strongylodon macrobotrys*) is only found in the wild in the rainforests of the Philippines. It was first seen by westerners in 1854. It can grow up to 18 metres (almost 60 ft) long, but it's the flowers that are the extraordinary part of this woody vine.

The waxy, claw-like flowers are an ethereal, almost luminous, blue-green colour and hang down in trusses of up to 90 flowers. They are very distinctive and have a shape similar to many other plants in the pea family (Fabaceae), but they have special modifications that allow them to be pollinated by bats.

Bats visit the pendant flowers to drink the copious nectar inside. As they hang upside down on the flowers they pull down the outer petal. This reveals the nectar, but also exposes the anthers and stigma (the plant's reproductive parts). A bat's head will get covered in pollen from the anthers while it devours the nectar. The bat then passes the pollen on to the next flower it visits, thereby fertilising it.

The rainforests where the jade vine grows are under severe threat, and this species is considered vulnerable to extinction in the wild. Research into the floral biology of this stunning plant is ongoing at the Royal Botanic Gardens, Kew, in order to help its conservation. Until 1995 jade vines at Kew had never produced seed, but detailed analysis of its flower structure revealed how best to pollinate it so that fertile seeds develop. The experiment was so successful, the resulting seed pods had to be supported by a net as they were so heavy.

Joshua Tree

A giant of the Mojave Desert, the Joshua tree is actually a species of yucca, *Yucca brevifolia*. It is superb at surviving in this arid environment – it has tough evergreen leaves, a deep root system, and is unusual in that it can grow very rapidly for a desert plant. It has a distinctive shape, which is said to be what inspired its common name, as Mormon settlers thought it looked like Joshua from the Bible raising his hands up to Heaven.

This tree relies on a particular group of moths (*Tegeticula* spp.), known as yucca moths, to pollinate its flowers. The female moth collects pollen from the flowers and stores it behind her head. She then seeks out a freshly opened flower and lays her eggs into or near the flower's ovary, while also depositing her collected pollen onto the stigma of the flower. This ensures pollination of the yucca flowers, which means that her larvae can then eat the developing yucca seeds in order to grow and complete their life cycle.

It is predicted that climate change will have a big impact on the Joshua tree, as it is hard for it to expand north as the climate warms. This is mainly due to the fact that the animals that once dispersed its seeds are now extinct – including the enormous shasta ground sloth. The Joshua tree, along with its moth partner, will probably need help from people in moving to more suitable areas in the future.

JUNIPER

You may know the common juniper (*Juniperus communis*) as a very spiky, scrubby-looking conifer, but don't forget that juniper berries are essential in producing the distinctive flavour of gin, so it's a very useful plant to have around. It grows wild across the northern hemisphere, and is one of only three conifers thought to be native to Great Britain.

The 'berries' used in gin making are actually fleshy cones, which take two years to mature slowly on the plant turning from green to black. They were also once used in herbal medicine, as an astringent and carminative for stomach and digestive ailments, as well in topical treatments for joint and muscle pain. However, juniper must be used with care as it can cause extreme irritation when ingested and can lead to kidney and bladder problems. It was once also used to induce abortions. 'Savin' is an old name for juniper, and giving birth 'under the savin tree' was a euphemism for a miscarriage or a juniper-induced abortion.

Today, the common juniper is becoming less common in the UK, as populations are declining due to changes in grazing and land management, and also because of a soil-borne fungus (*Phytophthora austrocedrae*) that can kill these plants. Organisations such Plantlife and Trees for Life, among others, are helping to restore native juniper populations while the Millennium Seed Bank at the Royal Botanic Gardens, Kew, is collecting seed from several populations in England to help study how best to germinate these hardy little trees and conserve them for the future.

Did you know? As juniper wood gives off little smoke when it is burned, it is said that it was once the fuel of choice in illicit whisky stills in the Scottish Highlands!

Just Buzz In

Some plants can afford to be picky about their pollinators – choosing not only which insect can take their nectar and pollen, but also when that happens. Buzz pollination (or sonication) is a good example of this.

Most insects can't access the pollen of plants who employ this tactic as the pollen is hidden inside a tube-like anther, but several types of bee, including bumblebees, have a particular trick to help release it. The female bees produce vibrations against the anthers which are at just the right frequency and duration to release a cloud of nutritious pollen that the bee then collects. The bee uses this for food, but some will also be transferred onto the flowers of the same plant species to pollinate it.

It is thought that up to 20,000 plant species employ this tactic, including many economically important plants such as tomatoes and aubergines, blueberries and cranberries. More spectacular examples are found in certain species of *Gustavia* from the Amazon and Guianas. These neo-tropical forest trees have flowers that first open at night, and night-flying bees are the principal pollinators of these large cauliflorous flowers (which emerge from the main stem or trunk rather than from new growth or shoots). A tuning fork placed on the flower produces the same resonance as the bee and causes a dramatic release of pollen.

is for...

KALE, CABBAGES, BROCCOLI AND SPROUTS

Did you know that cabbage, kale, Brussels sprouts, kohlrabi, cauliflower and broccoli are all cultivated varieties (cultivars) of a single plant species? Step up *Brassica oleracea*, also known as wild cabbage. Native to southern and western Europe, it can be found growing in coastal areas. It has been cultivated and eaten as a winter vegetable since at least Roman times, and has been bred into such diverse forms since then that the resulting crops are now hardly recognisable as being so closely related.

Each different cultivar of the species was selected by farmers over many generations, using plants with the particular desired characteristics to propagate new seedlings, gradually resulting in the completely different-looking vegetables. For example, cabbages were selected to produce many leaves from a single terminal vegetative bud to form a tight round 'head'. Kale was selected to produce numerous large leaves, and Brussels sprouts to produce many lateral vegetative buds, each one forming a single sprout on a long stem. Kohlrabi was selected to produce a single thick, short stem. Cauliflower was selected to produce its flowers in one large head – the white part of cauliflower is lots of unopened flower buds – whereas broccoli was selected to produce more separate flower clusters and longer stems.

Most of these cultivars are now promoted as 'superfoods' as they are rich in nutrients, vitamins and minerals, which all add up to being extremely good for your health. Broccoli is said to enhance heart health and protect against cancer.

Katsura Caramels

Katsura trees (*Cercidiphyllum japonicum*) are some of the most ornamental trees you could wish for – they have delicate heart-shaped leaves that are pink in spring, turn green in summer and then change to a mixture of orange-red and yellow in autumn. However, they also have a very special quality that makes them even more desirable – in autumn their leaves smell of candyfloss or burnt sugar. The scent is caused by the breakdown of maltol in the leaves – the same molecule you'll find in caramel. It is not yet known why this molecule exists in the leaves of this species.

Killer Tomatoes

You might think you'd know a carnivorous plant by looking at it – most have traps full of digestive juices or sticky leaves to catch prey with – but in 2009 scientists from the Royal Botanic Gardens, Kew, discovered hundreds more types of plants that are making a meal of insects and small invertebrates. Surprisingly, these include many harmless-looking plants that most of us have in our veg plots such as tomatoes (*Solanum lycopersicum*) and potatoes (*Solanum tuberosum*), as well as pretty ornamentals such as petunias.

These plants have sticky hairs on their stems or leaves. These were usually regarded as a defence against herbivores, but they also trap insects which, unable to escape, die and fall to the soil where they decompose and can be absorbed by the plant – a kind of passive carnivory.

One of the strangest examples the scientists discovered was the shepherd's purse (*Capsella bursa-pastoris*), which has carnivorous seeds. As the seeds absorb water, before germination, they produce a slimy mucilage that attracts soil invertebrates, but it also contains toxins that kill them. The seeds secrete an enzyme that can then help absorb the nutrients surrounding it, benefiting its growth into a seedling.

Even the most innocent-looking plants may have something sinister to hide …

Kissable Lips

In the tropical forests of Central and South America there is an attractive plant that looks as if it's begging for a kiss. It's been compared to Angelina Jolie and Mick Jagger, and is reminiscent of Salvador Dali's *Mae West Lips* sofa.

Just prior to flowering *Psychotria elata* grows two large waxy red bracts (modified leaves), which pucker up and for all the world look like two large red lips. The resemblance is reasonably short-lived unfortunately as the bracts then open and several star-shaped white flowers emerge from between them. Its appearance has earned the plant the common names of 'hot lips' and 'hooker's lips'. However, it isn't a great idea to kiss this sensuous-looking plant as it contains psychoactive alkaloids. Some indigenous peoples have used it for treating a variety of ailments (including snakebites) and also in midwifery.

This understorey shrub is a member of the coffee family (Rubiaceae) and is mainly pollinated by hummingbirds. The red bracts are flags to the birds to come to visit the tubular nectar-filled flowers, and once pollinated, tiny, round blue-ish fruits develop. This astonishing species is sadly under threat from deforestation in its native habitat.

Koteka

Penis gourds, known as koteka or phyllocrypts, are a traditional part of New Guinea culture and dress in the highlands of the islands. Dried-out gourds (usually *Lagenaria siceraria*, the bottle or calabash gourd) are worn over the penis by traditional tribesmen. To make them the correct size and shape the gourds are manipulated as they are grown, using weights and strings tied in different directions to guide their growth.

Usually a loop of fibre is used to secure the base of the koteka around the scrotum, or it may be held on by friction alone, and another length of fibre is wrapped around the waist and attached to the end of the gourd. Koteka may be used as a purse to hold small items such as money or cigarettes, and may be worn every day as part of normal attire or reserved for ceremonial reasons.

Different tribes prefer different shapes, and the gourds may be held at different angles by adjusting the tying of the tip from straight up through to straight out. The koteka may be decorated with feathers or paintings, and different sizes and shapes worn, but the length of the gourd used is not considered to be related to the status of the wearer. Whether or not a man wears one at all may be related to their societal role, perhaps as an unmarried bachelor or a married father. Wearing a gourd in this way has been reported in Latin America and Africa as well, and a whole body of research literature exists on the gourd species used and how the practice of wearing the gourds may have spread across the globe in pre-Colombian times.

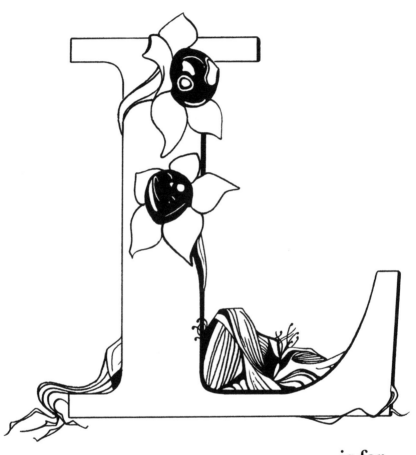

is for...

LARGEST SEED

The largest and heaviest seed of any plant in the world is produced by the coco-de-mer palm (*Lodoicea maldivica*), also known as the double coconut or Seychelles nut (after its native island). The mature seed can weigh anything between 15 and 30 kg (33–66 lb), and it can be up to an astonishing 50 cm (over 1.6 ft) long.

The fruit that contains the seed requires six to seven years to mature on the tree, and once released from the parent plant the seed may take up to two years to germinate. It is thought the seeds are so big in order to help the seedling be as competitive as possible in the forest. The bi-lobed seed is instantly recognisable by its suggestive shape, said to resemble a human bottom!

The coco-de-mer palm is endemic to the Seychelles, and only around 8,000 mature individuals exist. Although protected, the species is classed as endangered. It is truly unique as it has the largest female flowers of any palm, and has some of the largest leaves and flowers of any plant in the world.

LAST OF THE ROMANTICS

Medicines are often poisonous if the dose given is incorrect – this is true for 'natural' plant-derived chemicals as much as it is for synthetically-produced drugs. Plant derivatives are also administered for all sorts of non-medicinal purposes, including cosmetic and recreational uses. Unfortunately, there have been instances where this kind of use has been at poisonous levels too.

Atropa belladonna is commonly known as belladonna, literally 'beautiful lady' in Italian, or by its more sinister name – deadly nightshade. A member of the Solanaceae (the same family as tomatoes, aubergines, potatoes and peppers), plants in this family often contain high levels of toxic chemicals, especially in the leaves and fruits.

The drug atropine, originally derived from belladonna, is now used in eye surgery to cause the pupils to dilate. From Roman times through to the Victorian era, juice from the berries of belladonna was used as eye drops for ladies – not for eye surgery but to induce the same dilation of the pupils. These large, watery pupils were considered to be extremely beautiful, romantic and seductive.

Unfortunately, applying a potent poison to your eyes too frequently can lead to a range of unpleasant symptoms including heart arrhythmia, hallucinations, blurred vision and ultimately blindness, and is occasionally fatal.

Other potentially deadly members of the Solanaceae include *Datura* and *Brugmansia* (see **Z is for Zombies**), *Mandragora* (mandrake) (see **M is for Magical Mandragora**) and *Nicotiana* (tobacco). These plants all contain toxic alkaloids called tropanes, some of the strongest drugs known in terms of their effect on the human nervous system.

LATEX

Natural rubber starts out as a milky fluid called latex, which drips from the damaged trunks of the Pará rubber tree (*Hevea brasiliensis*), deep in the forests of South America. This thick sticky substance helps to protect the tree from herbivores, and is actually produced by many plants – particularly, but not exclusively, those in the family Euphorbiaceae.

Rubber made from a range of plants was used by Mesoamericans for over 3,000 years, and Spanish colonialists reported the use of latex to waterproof clothing and even sandals. But it was little known in Europe until as recently as 150 years ago.

Charles Macintosh was one of the first Europeans to make use of natural rubber's waterproofing qualities. The Scot lent his name to the eponymous raincoats by sticking together two layers of fabric dipped in liquid rubber with an inner layer of rubber, producing the first marketable waterproof fabric.

Another Charles, Goodyear, in the USA, was experimenting at the same time as Thomas Hancock in the UK, trying to overcome the problems that occurred when natural rubber became either too hot or too cold. When too hot, rubber becomes sticky and unusable; too cold and it becomes brittle. More or less simultaneously, Goodyear and Hancock discovered that heating rubber with lead and sulphur, in a process called vulcanisation, produced a much more stable, long-lasting material that did not react so badly in extremes of temperature.

Other useful latex-producing plants include several species of *Manilkara* and *Palaquium*, both in the Sapotaceae family. 'Chicle', derived from *Manilkara*, was chewed by the Aztecs and Mayans, and used by the Wrigley Chewing Gum Company until they switched to synthetic forms of chewing rubber or 'gum'. *Palaquium* produces a latex called 'gutta-percha' – a more rigid form of rubber, which was used extensively for underwater telegraph cabling prior to the advent of synthetic polymers.

Carl von Linné, as he was known in his native Swedish, or Carolus Linnaeus in Latin (the language of science in his day), is referred to today as the 'Father of Taxonomy'. Spending much of his scientific career at the Swedish University of Uppsala, Linnaeus formalised the binomial system of classifying and naming plants that we still use today.

The binomial system comprises the two parts of every Latin plant name. The first part assigns the species to a specific genus (a group of the most closely related species in a plant family, linked by common ancestry, and which often show similar characteristics). For example, all species of rose are more closely related to each other than they are to any other species, and are in the same genus, *Rosa*.

The second part of a plant's species name is called the 'specific epithet'. This is chosen by the botanist who formally publishes the species and may refer to a particular character of the species (such as hairiness or flower colour), to a geographic location where the plant is from, or be a dedication to another person (see **F is for Famous Names**). The specific epithet of the dog rose is *canina*, meaning 'dog' in Latin, so the complete binomial name for the species is *Rosa canina* – distinguishing the species from any others.

Linnaeus made a huge contribution to all areas of nomenclature and classification of the natural world, and published enormous tomes including *Systema Naturae, Genera Plantarum* and *Species Plantarum* on the hierarchical classification of organisms into kingdoms, classes, orders, genera, species and varieties. He divided the thousands of then known plants into species and genera based on natural characteristics – usually their reproductive structures.

Over 250 years later, Linnaeus' systems and the rules he devised still form the basis of the names and organisation of species used today.

LONGEST-LIVED LEAVES

In the unforgiving heat of the Namib Desert, where the only moisture comes from a fog that rolls in off the sea every day, there lives a remarkable plant. It only has two leaves, which grow continuously throughout its life, becoming torn and twisted as they age. It bears cones on separate male and female plants and uses wind pollination to reproduce. This is the tree tumbo or *Welwitschia mirabilis*, a plant so odd that it was described by Darwin as the 'platypus of the plant world'.

Where many plants have evolved tiny waxy leaves to conserve water in this desert environment, the tree tumbo has two large flat leathery leaves that snake across the rocky, sandy ground. It exposes a large surface area to the fog to grab as much moisture as it can. On the rare occasion when rain does fall, the plant grows rapidly. This strategy is precarious however, as should it lose one of its leaves it usually dies. Tree tumbos only grow these two leaves in their lifetime, and as they can live for around 500–600 years or longer, this makes them the longest-lived leaves known in the plant kingdom.

Lotus Effect

Place a drop of water on a lotus leaf (*Nelumbo nucifera*), a taro (*Colocasia esculenta*) or even a nasturtium (*Tropaeolum*) or lady's mantle (*Alchemilla mollis*), and you'll notice a strange occurrence. The droplet doesn't sink in, it stays perfectly formed and rolls around until sliding off the leaf, which remains dry.

This phenomenon is called 'superhydrophobicity' and doesn't just repel water from the leaves – the droplets also pick up dust, bacteria, and fungal spores as they roll around, helping the leaves to 'self-clean'. This is known as the 'Lotus Effect'.

The hydrophobic nature of such leaves is due to a range of microscopic structures in the epidermis of the leaf and a continuous layer of nano-sized wax crystals that create a very rough surface on the leaf and form an effective barrier. This was only discovered after the invention of the modern scanning electron microscope, which allowed scientists to see such minute detail.

Many plants have this ability to repel water to some degree; especially those from the tropics and subtropics. Much research has been done in recent years as to how to mimic this self-cleaning natural phenomenon for man-made products such as glass, paints, fabrics and other surfaces.

is for...

MAGICAL MANDRAGORA

Recognition of the need to identify plants goes back a long way. Many ancient books called 'herbals' identified and listed the uses of plants, but were also full of fanciful plants and bizarre illustrations. One of the most notorious plants to have had this treatment is the mandrake (*Mandragora officinarum*).

Some books contain images of the mandrake with its forked, often twisted taproots looking like little men or women ready to cast a spell over you. Over the centuries this plant has been used both for treating illnesses and trying to create them in others! It has also been used to try to forecast the future and to protect people from witches (see **W is for Witches and Warlocks**).

In the Middle Ages, mandrake was used for inducing sleep. It was an ingredient in concoctions with other plant extracts including opium and henbane, used to bring on a sleep that would allow surgery to take place. This species is now known to contain active alkaloids, including scopolamine – also known as 'devil's breath'. The alkaloids in mandrake can have a variety of powerful effects on people – from hallucinations and intoxication to unconsciousness.

Owing to these effects, mandrake was apportioned spiritual powers and magical properties, and these tales follow it to this day. It makes many appearances in literature, including Shakespeare's *Romeo and Juliet* and J. K. Rowling's *Harry Potter and the Chamber of Secrets* – where its scream is so loud when you uproot it that you must wear ear-defenders or risk being overwhelmed, sent to sleep, or even possibly killed.

While its roots were perhaps viewed with suspicion, its fruits were called 'apples of love', and in some stories they are used to create love potions. Make of that what you will.

BOTANY HERO

BARBARA McCLINTOCK (1902–1992)

Barbara McClintock was awarded the Nobel Prize in Physiology for her pioneering work on discovering 'mobile genetic elements', otherwise known as transposable elements or 'jumping genes'. In the 1940s and 1950s, McClintock studied how they operate in plant cells and are involved in the heredity of plant traits.

Transposable elements are genes (or groups of genes) that are able to change position on a chromosome, sometimes causing other genes to be switched on or off. Using maize (*Zea mays*), as her main study organism, McClintock unravelled the heredity of changes producing specific traits such as multi-coloured kernels.

Ahead of her time, discovering and describing radical new theories of genetic inheritance, McClintock's work was not fully appreciated until the 1960s and 1970s when other scientists began to investigate and verify her work. When she won the Nobel Prize in 1983, she was the first woman in history to have been awarded it in the category of Physiology or Medicine as a solo award, rather than as part of a team. The only other woman to have achieved this since has been Youyou Tu in 2015 for her work on treating malaria.

MEGADIVERSE MADAGASCAR

Madagascar is one of the hottest biodiversity hotspots on Earth. Renowned for its fauna, including lemurs and chameleons, this island is also famous for its flora – from striking baobabs in the genus *Adansonia* (see **U is for Upside-Down Trees**) to Darwin's comet orchid *Angraecum sesquipedale* (see **A is for Angraecum Associations**).

Of the approximately 14,000 plant species known from Madagascar, it is thought that as high a proportion as 90 per cent are likely to be endemic to the island – that is, found nowhere else on Earth (see **U is for (The Incredible) Uniqueness of Endemism**).

Unfortunately, threats to Madagascar's unique habitats and species are huge, and put increasing pressure on their existence. Less than 10 per cent of Madagascar's original vegetation is thought to remain, and the rates of soil erosion on the island are phenomenal – up to 400 tonnes (440 US tons) of soil lost per hectare, per year – a rate unmatched anywhere else on Earth.

A recent study of the palms of Madagascar showed that of the approximately 200 species known to grow on the island, 98 per cent are endemic, and 83 per cent are threatened with extinction (see **R is for Red Alert!**). Half of all endemic palms on Madagascar are known from just a single location, or have fewer than 50 individuals left in the wild. Nearly 1,000 orchid species are found on Madagascar, and approximately 90 per cent of those are thought to be endemic, and it is feared that the proportion of species threatened with extinction will be similarly high.

Time is running out for many Malagasy species, but a huge amount of groundbreaking, community-linked conservation work on Madagascar's flora and natural resources is going on, hopefully stemming and even reversing many of the potential losses.

Botany Hero
Archibald Menzies (1754–1842)

One of several important Scottish plant hunters in the late 18th century, Archibald Menzies is perhaps best known as the man who allegedly pilfered monkey puzzle tree seeds from his dessert at a presidential banquet in Santiago and subsequently introduced this stately tree (*Araucaria araucana*) to Great Britain. This is unfortunate as Menzies should be known for so much more for than this supposed sleight of hand.

Menzies travelled the world as a surgeon-naturalist in the Royal Navy. He circumnavigated the world twice visiting, among other countries, Australia, Madagascar and South America, and made many botanical discoveries. He was given the task of plant collecting by the great naturalist and unofficial director of Kew, Sir Joseph Banks. He also joined HMS *Discovery* under Captain George Vancouver, on an epic journey to the north-west coast of America in the 1790s.

To reflect the fact that Menzies was an extremely diligent plant collector, a genus of plants, *Menziesia*, is named after him, while nearly 100 plant taxa have been given the epithet menziesii, including *Pseudotsuga menziesii* – and *Nothofagus menziesii* – the Douglas fir and the southern beech – both of which he was the first to discover. The first official director of Kew, Sir William Hooker, cited over 190 species as being discovered by Menzies.

As for the monkey puzzle tree, it seems Menzies did recount this tale to Sir William's son, Joseph, later in life. Menzies was said to have brought back five seedling monkey puzzle trees for Sir Joseph Banks, one of which lived at Kew for almost a century, where it was known as the Joseph Banks' pine.

Mimicry, Sex and Violence

Orchids are notorious for being mimics – deceiving insects into pollinating them, while giving nothing in return. European bee orchids (*Ophrys*) are classic examples – luring male bees in with a modified petal, called the labellum, which resembles the female bee. Some species even emit a scent similar to the sex pheromones of female insects, proving irresistible to the males. Once a male lands on a flower, the furriness of the specialised labellum convinces him that this is a female bee and he continues with his mating behaviour. Instead of finding love however, he simply inadvertently collects pollen and ends up taking it to the next imposter he falls for.

The bizarre-looking hammer orchids (*Drakaea*) have a similar trick that works on thynnid wasps in Western Australia. The male wasp tries to grab the fake female (the labellum of the flower, modified to mimic the appearance of a female wasp) to fly off with her to mate, but instead only achieves having a sticky packet of pollen stuck to him, which he then unwittingly carries to the next hammer orchid, delivering it to that orchid's stigma and pollinating the flower.

One orchid, however, goes for violence instead of sex. The Chinese dendrobium orchid (*Dendrobium sinense*), which grows on the Chinese island of Hainan, has been found to lure in hornets, which attack the red centres of its otherwise white flowers. Research confirmed that the orchids were releasing a scent remarkably similar to that of a distressed honeybee – one of the hornets' prey. The hornets are lured in, thinking they will find a vulnerable bee releasing an alarm signal, but instead their attack ends up pollinating the flower.

Montezuma

As the father of the last of the Aztec emperors, Montezuma I was surely the original chocoholic. According to Spanish records of the time, the emperor had over 40,000 'loads' of cocoa beans in his royal stores (one load being the amount a trader could carry in one backpack).

Every Aztec banquet included more than 50 jars of the foaming, hot drink 'cacahuatl'. This drink was reserved for the highest echelons of society and commoners who broke the prohibition were put to death. Montezuma drank his cacahuatl from vessels of fine gold at banquets before retiring to his quarters. There he was served many different forms of the drink, mixed and flavoured with honey, vanilla, allspice, chilli pepper, flowers and other variations.

The basic recipe and preparation remain virtually unchanged today in modern Mexico, with toasted cocoa beans being ground to a sticky paste and water added. The paste is filtered, strained and aerated repeatedly, to create a thick and highly prized foam on top. At the time of Montezuma there was no sugar available, and although honey was sometimes added, the Aztecs found the bitterness of the raw cacao used entirely palatable.

The tree upon which cocoa beans grow, *Theobroma cacao* – meaning 'food of the gods' in Latin – is a member of the mallow family (Malvaceae) along with okra, cotton and hibiscus, and the fruits are technically berries, rather than beans or pods. Originally from tropical America, today more than two thirds of the world's commercial cocoa production is in West Africa.

Cocoa contains phenols and flavonoids whose antioxidant effects are thought to perhaps inhibit cancer and cardiovascular diseases. The theobromine and caffeine alkaloids also found in cocoa stimulate the central nervous system, improving mental alertness, and as with the caffeine in coffee, have an addictive effect – maybe at the root of Montezuma's famous penchant for the bean.

MUD-LOVING MANGROVES

Mangrove swamps are unlikely to win any plant beauty pageants, but their value is truly extraordinary. They occupy the ever-changing intertidal world of the tropical coastline: sometimes they are mainly submerged underwater, other times they stand naked in the baking salty mud.

Mangrove swamps occur worldwide, most extensively in Asia. Although they tend to only grow in narrow strips that fringe the coastline, they are some of the most productive habitats on Earth. Many species live together to form a 'mangrove forest', but there are also trees specifically called mangroves too; these belong to the genera *Rhizophora* and *Avicennia*. They are great examples of 'halophytes' – being highly adapted to an extreme salt-laden environment.

Many species in this habitat have adapted to excrete salt from their cells or to dilute its effects. The seeds of the red mangrove (*Rhizophora mangle*) germinate while they are still attached to the parent plant (known as vivipary); these can then float away, unaffected by the sea water, to establish new populations on other shores.

Mangroves use stilt-like 'pneumatophore' roots (see **P is for Pneumatophore Knees**) to stand high above the water and to help them respire in the waterlogged oxygen-starved mud. The tangled root systems that they create act as a safe haven for young fish, many crab species and shellfish, while the forests are also home to many species of birds, reptiles, amphibians, mammals and insects.

Mangroves are a vital part of a healthy marine ecosystem. Most importantly, perhaps, they protect the coastline from erosion. All of these things also protect the livelihoods of local people – from fisherman to those involved in local tourism, and the forests offer valuable resources for them. According to a recent WWF report the goods and services offered by mangrove forests are worth US$ 186 million per year to the world economy.

is for...

Neem

The demand for natural ingredients in our cosmetics continues to rise, but some plants have been used in this way for generations. One example is the seed oil and dried leaves of the tree *Azadirachta indica* – commonly known as neem – long used in Indian traditional medicine, as well as to protect stored foods and fabrics from insect damage.

You can find many products that have neem in their ingredients today including toothpaste, soap and moisturisers. It is sometimes paired with turmeric and sesame or coconut oil in cosmetic products to increase its effectiveness. A recent study has been investigating whether nimbolide, a compound found in neem leaves, can be used to treat pancreatic cancer.

The neem tree is a member of the mahogany family (Meliaceae), and is native to Bangladesh, India, Burma and Pakistan. Scientists from the Royal Botanic Gardens, Kew, identified a special chemical in neem that prevents insects from feeding and reproducing properly. This has since been made into a commercial insecticide product.

BOTANY HERO

LADY DOROTHY NEVILL (1826–1913)

Lady Dorothy Nevill was no stranger to great gardens and influential people; her father was the politician and art historian Horace Walpole and her mother was a friend of the Empress of Russia. Born in 1826, Lady Dorothy received no formal education, but had a voracious appetite for knowledge, especially for all things botanical.

In 1847 she married Reginald Nevill and they acquired a 800-hectare-estate (2,000 acres) in Sussex called Dangstein. You would be hard pressed to find someone who had heard of this estate now, but in its day the garden that Lady Dorothy created there once had more plants than the Royal Botanic Gardens, Kew.

Records show that the nine-hectare (23 acres) garden had parterres, a pinetum, some of the first herbaceous borders in the country, 17 glasshouses housing peaches, palms, orchids, vines, ferns and insectivorous plants, with tanks for waterlilies and other aquatic plants. Lady Dorothy managed to bring together species of plants that no-one else had, and Kew's director, Sir William Hooker (see H, Botany Hero: Hooker), was so impressed by her knowledge and the collections that he wrote to her several times to ask for specimens for Kew. Even the great scientist Charles Darwin (see D, Botany Hero: Charles Darwin) requested plants from her for his research.

Lady Dorothy had a wide circle of intellectual friends including the Prime Minister Benjamin Disraeli but, sadly, when her husband died in 1878 she had to sell the estate and all its plant collections. It is said she hoped these would go to Kew, but funds could not be raised, and many of the collections were taken abroad to the royal gardens of Monaco and Belgium.

NETTLE CLOTH

Would it surprise you to know that the stinging nettle (*Urtica dioica*) was once one of the most highly prized plants for making cloth? Excavation of a Bronze Age round barrow in 1861 on the Danish island of Funen revealed a cloth that was 2,800 years old. Originally thought to be linen, research determined the shroud was actually made of nettle, despite there being many other plants around at the time that cloth could be made from.

Nettles contain long fibres perfect for making high-quality fabric, and Bronze Age people chose to use it in some instances rather than anything else, despite the obvious pain of collecting it. The use of nettle for making fabrics continues to this day; it was even used by the German army for making uniforms in the First World War.

NOBLE RHUBARB

Most alpine plants are tiny, compact affairs, only really noticeable when they put out showy flowers for a brief time, once the snows have melted. The noble rhubarb (*Rheum nobile*), however, has gone for a completely different approach – it grows its own two-metre-tall greenhouse. It looks almost ridiculous, with large rhubarb-like leaves and a tall pale yellow column of bracts towering above other tiny species on the windswept scree slopes of the Himalayas, like a botanical lighthouse.

However, this species' solution to a challenging environment is ingenious, for the tall column of bracts protects a flower spike inside, trapping and warming the air around the flowers and protecting them from rain. On a sunny day the air inside the column is around 10°C (50°F) warmer than outside. This protection and warmth attracts gnats – the plant's pollinators – but also encourages seed development, resulting in larger seeds that are more likely to germinate.

Did you know? The original specimens collected by Sir Joseph Hooker in Sikkim in the late 1840s, and from which this species was described and given its name, can still be found in the Herbarium at the Royal Botanic Gardens, Kew.

NORTH'S INCREDIBLE PUYA

If ever a plant looked like it had landed from outer space, then *Puya berteroniana* is it. This extraordinary spiky-leaved bromeliad from Chile sends up flower spikes that can reach up to 3.5 metres (11.5 ft) high. Each is packed with astonishingly vibrant blue-green flowers, in the centre of which are bright orange anthers. Sticking out at wild angles from this column of flowers are yellow spikelets, which give the plant a slightly crazed look. It's the kind of sight that makes you stop in your tracks.

The flowers are attractive to birds who come to drink their nectar, getting their heads daubed with yellow pollen as they do so and pollinating the flowers as they feed.

One of the first people to record this species in flower in its natural habitat was the intrepid Victorian painter Marianne North, in 1884. She described her climb to see them in the Cordilleras Mountains in her journal: 'Behold, just over my head, a great group of noble flowers, standing out like ghosts at first, then gradually coming out with their full beauty and form.' You can still see her oil paintings of this astonishing plant in the Marianne North Gallery at the Royal Botanic Gardens, Kew, today.

Did you know? Another species of *Puya* from Chile – *Puya chilensis* – has such incredible spikes that it can ensnare birds and animals. It is known locally as the 'sheep-eating-plant'.

is for...

OLDEST FRUITS

Preserved for 32,000 years and discovered in the permafrost of the Siberian tundra, the fruits of the narrow-leaved campion (*Silene stenophylla*) are the oldest viable flowering plant material known to date. More amazing is that in 2012 tissue from these ancient fruits was used to grow new living plants.

Russian scientists had first tried to germinate seeds found at the same site, but found that they were not viable, possibly owing to damage by the squirrels thought to have collected and buried the plant material all those years ago. Only when they tried to use tissue from the immature fruits, rather than the seeds, were they able to produce living plants. These looked virtually identical to modern-day *Silene stenophylla* plants as they grew, but when they flowered, subtle but clear distinctions between the ancient and modern-day variants were evident. The ancient plants had narrower petals with less clearly dissected ends, and some of the flowers on each plant produced female parts only, rather than all flowers being bisexual, as in the modern-day *Silene stenophylla*.

We know that cryopreservation – storing plant material at extreme sub-zero temperatures – is a very effective way of retaining viability of cells for growth in the future, while preventing deleterious degradation and mutation of DNA. Studies of naturally cryopreserved sites such as the permafrost of the Arctic tundra are revealing more and more ancient organisms, from plants to viruses, held in a sort of 'suspended animation', with the potential to be regenerated like these ancient *Silene* plants.

Oldest Pot Plant in the World

The Eastern Cape giant cycad (*Encephalartos altensteinii*) growing in the Palm House at Kew is one of the oldest pot plants in the world. Collected in the Eastern Cape region of South Africa in the early 1770s, it was brought back to England by boat in 1775 by Francis Masson, Kew's first plant collector. Masson had been sent to South Africa on a plant-hunting mission by the famous naturalist Sir Joseph Banks – Kew's unofficial first director.

Today, this ancient-looking plant resides in a large mahogany planter, propped up with metal supports, in the steamy environs of the Palm House. It measures almost four and half metres from the base of its stem to the growing point (with an average growth rate of only 2.5 cm or an inch per year). During its time at Kew it has only produced one cone, which Banks came to see on his final visit to Kew before his death in 1820.

Did you know? The cycad family pre-dates flowering plants, and is a botanical throwback to the days of the dinosaurs, producing large cones rather than flowers. They are a very primitive type of plant and can live for 500 years or longer and provide botanists with clues as to what early plant life was like.

On Her Majesty's Secret Service

Botanists don't often appear in popular fiction, but Ian Fleming – the author and creator of James Bond, 007 himself – once happened to meet the head of the orchid herbarium at the Royal Botanic Gardens, Kew, Victor Summerhayes, and was so taken with the meeting that he wrote him into his next book, *On Her Majesty's Secret Service*.

Summerhayes was described as 'the orchid king at Kew', and in the book M describes the mycorrhizal relationships between orchids and the fungal symbionts that infect their roots – and, in his spare time, is revealed to paint the wild orchids of England in watercolours to relax.

Kew popped up again in the next of Fleming's books, *You Only Live Twice*, and a poisonous (and completely fictitious) black orchid from the Amazon rainforest was featured in the film of *Moonraker.*

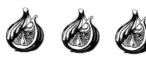

ORCHIDS TAKE OVER THE WORLD

If every seed produced by a single orchid plant were to germinate, and every seed produced by each of those plants germinated too, and so on, the 'great-grandchildren' of the original plant would cover the entire surface of the planet – with no room for anything or anyone else.

This sounds like a ridiculous theory, belonging to the world of *The Day of the Triffids*, but Charles Darwin (see **D, Botany Hero: Charles Darwin**) was perplexed about this very problem. Recognising that orchid species often produced huge numbers of their tiny dust-like seed in each seed capsule, Darwin estimated the total number of seeds (and therefore individual progeny) a single plant of *Orchis maculata* could produce in a single generation.

With each plant producing over 180,000 seeds, he calculated that if each plant took up a space six inches square in size, the first generation would fill an acre of land. The second generation would cover an area equivalent to the island of Anglesey, and the third generation would clothe the entire planet.

Yet, obviously, the surface of the Earth is not covered with orchids, and Darwin specifically noted that orchids were notoriously 'sparingly distributed'. He knew that something must be keeping the enormous reproductive potential of such species in check, but he did not know what it was.

Today, we know that one of the major reasons why most orchid seed never germinates is because orchids depend on a particular fungal partner being present where the seed lands. If an appropriate fungus is present, the seed is able to form a mycorrhizal association with it, germinate and ultimately develop into a mature plant. If the right fungus is not present, the seed cannot germinate, and it will die.

Oud

Oud, oudh, eaglewood, agarwood … there are many names for the dense, resin-rich wood of trees in the family Thymelaeaceae. The wood, and the oil extracted from it, has been used for thousands of years – and is highly valuable. Mostly found in species in the genus *Aquilaria*, but also *Gyrinops*, *Gonystylus* and a number of other genera, oud is produced in the heartwood of these trees in response to fungal attack. The tree's toxic resins, full of volatile compounds, fight off the invading fungi. These resins permeate the tree's woody tissues, turning them black-brown and making them stronger and more resilient to attack by the fungus in the process.

Trees in which this process occurs are much sought after as oud can be sold for high prices and is thought to be the most valuable timber in the world. The wood is often made into ceremonial and religious artefacts, including prayer beads and incense, as well as secular items including non-religious carvings, perfumes and medicines.

Because you cannot tell if a tree is infected with the fungus, and producing oud, until you cut it down and split it open, you cannot predict if a particular tree may contain this valuable product or not. As a result, many trees are cut down and vegetated habitats destroyed as a result of indiscriminate felling of potential oud-containing trees.

International trade of all oud-producing species is now strictly controlled and monitored by the Convention on International Trade in Endangered Species (CITES) to try and reduce this unsustainable, damaging harvesting. Attempts have been made to cultivate or semi-cultivate oud species by artificially inoculating trees with the fungus, to promote infection of the host and the subsequent production of the desired oud.

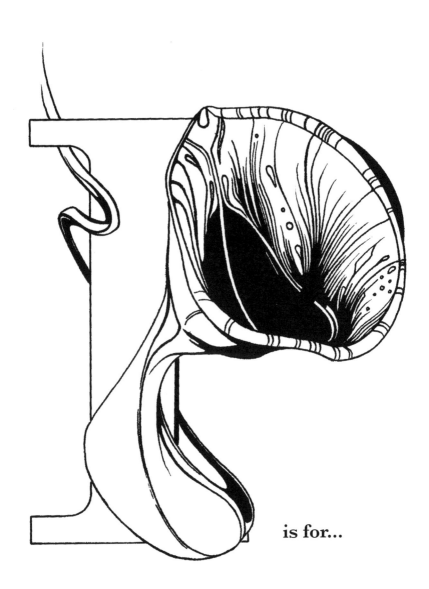

is for...

Paper Birch

If you ever find yourself trapped or abandoned in the North American wilderness on a Ray Mears-style adventure, it's worth looking out for the paper birch tree, *Betula papyrifera*, as it could well save your life.

The smooth whitish bark is waterproof as a result of its high oil content, which also means it is very flexible. It has been put to many uses including for canoes, paddles, tepees, water holders and baskets, as well as for making poultices or even casts for broken bones. It's also the perfect material for starting a campfire. The sweet inner bark can be eaten or boiled to make a drink.

As its common name suggests you can use the easily peelable bark to write home on too, although it might be a trek to the nearest post office.

Phytoestrogens: Friend or Foe?

Some of the food plants we consider to be healthy may actually have unwanted effects on the human body. A group of plant-derived compounds called phytoestrogens (thought to have a role in plant defence) are found in soy and other legumes, flaxseeds and brassicas such as kale, greens and broccoli. Phytoestrogens are widely reported to have a range of health benefits, for which there is an ever increasing body of scientific evidence. Phytoestrogens in your diet may lower your risk of osteoporosis, heart disease and some cancers.

But there is also evidence that in some people, some of these compounds could have adverse health effects, as in certain circumstances they are thought to have endocrine-disrupting effects – negatively interacting with the human hormone system.

Phytoestrogens seem to be structurally and functionally similar to mammalian hormones (oestrogens) and some are classed as goitrogens – substances that may promote the formation of a goitre (enlarged thyroid gland).

Although there is a lot of evidence that for the majority of people phytoestrogens are a beneficial part of a healthy diet, if you have a hormone-related condition (such as hypothyroidism, menopause symptoms or fertility-related problems) and you eat a lot of phytoestrogen-rich foods, it may be wise to discuss your condition and diet with your GP.

PINEAPPLE PARTY PIECES

The pineapple, *Ananas comosus*, arrived in Europe as long ago as 1493. Christopher Columbus is said to be the first European to have ever seen one.

Rich gentleman had special hothouses built in their gardens to try to grow the exotic pineapple and show off to each other. Even in the 17th century, pineapples were rare and expensive treats, and people would hire them to display at dinner parties. They became a symbol of wealth and welcome, and you can still see stone pineapples on the gateposts of historic houses today. The pineapple is the only bromeliad (member of the plant family Bromeliaceae) to be sold commercially on a large scale around the world.

Pitch Up and Poo

If you're familiar with pitcher plants (*Nepenthes*), you'll know they're famous for tricking hapless insects and even small mammals into falling into their jug-like traps, full of a digestive soup, from which their victims can't escape. This is all fairly standard carnivorous plant behaviour. However, there are some pitcher plants that have developed a much friendlier way of getting their dinner – by offering a quick snack or even a bed for the night.

Nepenthes lowii, from the cloud forests of Borneo, caught the headlines in 2009 when it was found to be attracting mountain tree shrews, who would balance on the rim of its sturdy pitchers to lick a sugary solution from the lid. The shrew then obligingly uses the pitcher as a toilet bowl. Its droppings contain valuable nutrients, thereby feeding the plant, supplying between half and all of the nitrogen it needs. The arrangement is mutually beneficial; the tree shrews value the pitchers so much that they scent-mark them to signal ownership.

Also in Borneo, as well as in Brunei, the long pitchers of *Nepenthes rafflesiana* var. *elongata* have been spotted offering accommodation to Hardwicke's woolly bats. The bats fit themselves neatly into the pitchers like they are sleeping bags, and take a nap during the day. They repay the plant for allowing them to stay by leaving droppings inside the pitcher.

Plant Clocks

Some of us feel that we need a few good cups of coffee in the morning before we are fighting fit and ready for the day, but new research has revealed that plants are at their very best first thing in the morning.

Scientists at the University of Warwick found that plants can predict when they are most likely to be attacked by fungal pathogens, and have their immune system ready and on high alert. The researchers discovered that a single protein in the plant's cells helped to link the plant's internal Circadian clock (which recognises night from day) to its immune system, allowing it to fight off the highest risk of infection at dawn. This research could have a huge impact in helping plant breeders to improve disease resistance in crop plants.

PNEUMATOPHORE KNEES

Also known as 'breathing knees', the extraordinary knobbly aerating root structures known as pneumatophores can be seen emerging from waterlogged, anaerobic soil around the base of certain species of trees, including the swamp cypress (*Taxodium distichum*), and many mangrove species such as *Avicennia germinans* and *Avicennia marina* (see **M is for Mud-Loving Mangroves**).

The pneumatophores help the plants to 'breathe'. The surface of these roots is packed with lenticels – 'pores' in the bark full of loosely packed cells, which allow for the easy exchange of gases for respiration.

is for...

Queen of the Night

Once a year, and for one night only, an unprepossessing cactus from Mexico and Central America becomes one of the most stunning floral exhibitionists in the plant world. It times its flowering with the full moon, opening a series of enormous, intricate yellow and white flowers in the hope of attracting bats.

As well as being beacons in the moonlight, the flowers of the queen of the night cactus (*Selenicereus grandiflorus*) release a vanilla-like scent to lure the bats in for a nectar feast and to hopefully pollinate the flowers at the same time.

The flowers only open for a matter of hours during the night and close when the sun rises, protecting them from the fierce heat of the day. Flowers of plants that grow in arid environments have to be amazingly colourful in order to attract their pollinators quickly, but flowering at night is also a key adaptation to help conserve moisture in the plant. Many cacti in Central America flower in time to coincide with an annual bat migration from Mexico to Arizona.

Quercus Qualities

Known as a symbol of strength and longevity, the English oak (*Quercus robur*) is one of best known and beloved tree species in Great Britain. It is easily recognisable by the distinctive shape of its leaves, and its acorns. The English oak's acorns sit on top of stalks, which distinguishes this species from the sessile oak (*Q. petraea*), whose acorns have no stalks.

One of the most notable things about oaks is the biodiversity associated with them. Mature oaks are thought to support more life than any other native tree species in Britain – around 500 species, including insects, birds, small mammals, fungi, lichens and even other plants such as mosses and ferns. Their acorns are rich in starch and provide food for jays, wood pigeons, mice and squirrels among other species, while an abundance of insects live on and around them including butterflies such as the purple hairstreak, and stag beetles. Several bat species are known to prefer to roost in oak trees.

More than 2,000 species of fungi are associated with oaks. Those commonly seen include the beefsteak fungus (*Fistulina hepatica*), the oakbug milkcap (*Lactarius quietus*) and the chicken of the woods (*Laetiporus sulphureus*).

The oak is at the centre of a web of biodiversity during its entire life (usually around 300 years, unless pollarded after which oaks can live over 1,000 years) *and* as it rots down after dying. It supports myriad species in a vast array of food chains across the forest. The oak has of course also been the source of many of the tools, furniture, building materials, weapons and ships that have played a key part of British history, industry and culture, making it one of the most useful and iconic species of this country.

Quickest Sucker

What bladderworts (*Utricularia* spp.) lack in looks they make up for in speed. These aquatic, rootless little plants are carnivorous and have little bladder-shaped suction traps, known for quickly sucking in small prey.

Each little bladder has four outer trigger hairs to alert it to passing creatures. The bladders pump out water with their trap doors firmly shut, for around an hour, creating negative pressure inside. Prey have only to brush a trigger hair and the door opens, sucking the hapless victim into the bladder in a swirling gush of water, where it is then slowly digested.

Researchers from the University of Grenoble used cameras that shoot 15,000 frames per second to document this process. They discovered that the trap doors open for less than a millisecond and the bladder sucks water in at an amazing acceleration of 600 times the force of gravity.

Quinine in your G&T

The bitter bark of the cinchona tree (the genus *Cinchona*), native to the Andean mountains, has passed into history as an essential component of both a traveller's medical supplies and their drinks cabinet. 'Quinquina' or quinine (the active ingredient found in the bark of the tree) was found to be a powerful anti-malarial back in the early 1600s by the Spanish Jesuits based in South America.

Increasingly, ships' doctors realised the importance of crews being given the drug when in tropical climes, and by the 1840s, the British were using 700 tonnes (770 US tons) of cinchona bark annually in India. Long supply routes from the eastern slopes of the Andes, and government monopolies, meant that exports of cinchona bark became more and more expensive and unpredictable.

In the 1860s seeds were taken to India by Kew botanists, where cinchona was grown in mountainous areas, and the resulting quinine distributed as cheaply as possible to local populations. In contrast, the Dutch East India Company focused on the global export market, based on growing cinchona in Java.

The combination of gin and tonic water developed out of the need to find a palatable way of consuming one's daily quinine ration. The bitter, unpleasant bark could be dried and ground, before being mixed with alcohol – into which the active alkaloids would readily dissolve. Mixing the tincture with soda water and sugar made what became known as a 'tonic water'. Since the officers of the British Raj tended to use gin to dissolve their quinine, the classic combination of gin and tonic water was born.

Quite Simply Quinoa

South American 'superfood' quinoa (*Chenopodium quinoa*) has surged in popularity over recent years. Closely related to beetroot, spinach and amaranth, it is a pseudo-cereal (true cereals being harvested from members of the grass family), protein-rich and highly nutritious. Although most quinoa is imported from the Andean countries from where it originates, it can also be successfully grown in the UK.

Historically, quinoa was cultivated by the Andean peoples over 3,000 years ago and it became one of their staple foods. The Incas deemed it so vital it was considered sacred, and they called it the 'mother grain'. It was added to soups and stews, as well as made into flour, and even fermented into a beer. Today, quinoa offers a valuable alternative source of quality protein, vitamins and minerals compared to some other cereals around the world, and is a very high-yielding crop. The seed coating contains bitter-tasting saponins, which handily puts off hungry birds, but has to be removed before the grain reaches consumers.

Quinoa is not only eaten as a grain, but can be found in a vast variety of products including breads, sweets, breakfast cereals, drinks and cakes. 2013 was named the International Year of Quinoa to celebrate its important role in eradicating malnutrition and food insecurity.

is for...

Raffles' Rafflesia

A rare, parasitic, rootless and leafless plant, *Rafflesia arnoldii* has the largest known flower in the world. Native to the jungles of Borneo and Sumatra, this species is truly bizarre. The main body of the plant resides inside another plant – a host – usually from the vine genus *Tetrastigma*, from the Vitaceae (the same plant family as grapes).

Rafflesia only reveals itself when it flowers. In a scene reminiscent of the film *Alien*, the flower buds burst through the host's bark and develop into a flower up to one metre (over three feet) in diameter. The red and orange-spotted flowers are quite revolting, resembling rotting flesh and emitting a foetid perfume to lure in carrion flies – earning it the common name corpse flower. The flies head towards the central cup-like structure of the flower where they get covered in pollen, but receive no reward for their help in pollinating the flower.

Little is known about the grapefruit-sized fruits that result from this pollination. It is thought that they may have been originally eaten and dispersed by Asian elephants, but these are rare in the habitats where *Rafflesia* grow today.

This unusual species is named after the two men who first collected it in 1818 – British botanist Joseph Arnold and Sir Thomas Raffles (the founder of modern Singapore). Many sites where *Rafflesia* grows are now popular with tourists, who provide an income for local people and also an incentive to preserve the species. Unfortunately, as a result of this ecotourism and the subsequent human disturbance, the number of flower buds produced per year has decreased significantly at many sites.

RED ALERT!

News stories and articles about imperiled plants and animals around the world, under threat from human activities such as deforestation or climate change, often use terms such as 'Vulnerable', 'Endangered' and 'Critically Endangered' in a very specific way.

These terms have particular meanings according to the IUCN Red List of Threatened Species guidelines, a rigorous set of rules that scientists use to assess species according to comparable criteria. Depending on the results, species are assigned an IUCN Red List extinction risk category – ranging from 'Least Concern' (the lowest category of risk) through to 'Critically Endangered' (the highest risk).

When an IUCN rating is given, it is important to understand that the assessment is based on the current knowledge of a species. This may change with new research, and threats may appear or disappear, so ideally species should be reassessed periodically. The rating is also based on the risk of that species becoming extinct within a short time frame, such as within a human lifetime. Without this second caveat most species (especially plants that are unable to rapidly relocate themselves) could be assessed as threatened with extinction because the vast majority will be negatively affected by future and ongoing climate change.

Recent work by researchers at the Royal Botanic Gardens, Kew, using a representative sample of plants, has shown that one in five of all plant species on Earth are likely to be threatened with extinction, having been assessed as one of the top three IUCN categories – Vulnerable, Endangered or Critically Endangered.

With limited resources, everywhere in the world, these rigorous, peer-reviewed assessments of extinction risk allow conservationists, politicians and funders to 'triage' species and prioritise those that appear to be the most threatened.

Resurrection

Some plants have really remarkable abilities. Those that get dubbed 'resurrection plants' are certainly among them. One of the most famous plants that goes by this moniker is *Selaginella lepidophylla*, also known as spikemoss. You can literally watch it come back to life from a shrivelled curled-up mass in just a matter of hours.

This species is a primitive plant, native to the Chihuahuan Desert (in North America), and has evolved an amazing adaptation to living in an arid environment among cacti and other succulents. In times of drought it cannot retain water so it slowly dries out; the stems of this flat rosette curl tightly in on themselves until the plant becomes a brown clam-like ball. The older outer stems protect the younger stems inside.

The plant then becomes metabolically dormant. Astonishingly, it can remain like this for years. However, this species has the ability to absorb water rapidly when it becomes available, its cells rehydrate quickly, the stems unfurl dramatically; it starts to turn green and the plant can begin to grow again.

Rose is a Rose, is a Rose, is a Rose

Roses (*Rosa* spp.) are not just beautiful additions to our gardens, they have an important place in our history and culture too. They have long been used in traditional medicines, but also in flavouring and preserving dishes, and of course in perfumes and even confetti. They have acted as symbols of love in poetry, music and literature, but also as political emblems. Their colour, taste, beauty and thorns have all found meaning in our culture.

But do all roses have thorns? Some 1980s rock ballads would have us believe so, but technically their sharp spikes are in fact *prickles*. 'Thorns' are modified stems that grow from a bud, whereas 'prickles' arise from anywhere on the stem's epidermis (its outer layer). The rose produces these for protection against browsing animals, but also to help it to climb upwards among other plants.

BOTANY HERO
GEORG EBERHARD RUMPHIUS
(1627–1702)

Rumphius must have been one of the unluckiest, and yet most persistent, botanists in history. Living on Ambon, in east Indonesia, for nearly 50 years until his death, the German-born Dutchman was employed by the Dutch East India Company.

Taking a keen interest in natural history and how the people of the Ambon archipelago lived in harmony with the natural world, Rumphius began documenting the huge diversity of native plants around him, and their uses. He went on to write the definitive record for the time of the plants of the Spice Islands, of which Ambon was one, in his enormous work the Ambon Herbal (or the *Herbarium Amboinense*).

This magnum opus almost never saw the light of day however, as an unusual number of misfortunes beset Rumphius. He was blinded by cataracts and glaucoma when he was about 42, after years of working by candlelight. His wife and youngest daughter were killed in an earthquake shortly thereafter. The manuscript was almost totally lost in a fire a few years later, and he had to rewrite it from memory, with the aid of scribes as his sight had failed completely by then.

The 'Blind Seer of Ambon' then faced further trials as the rewritten finished manuscript was lost at sea en route to the Netherlands after the ship was sunk by the French. Luckily a partial copy had been made at the request of Company officials, and with this Rumphius was able to salvage his work and rewrite it once again.

The final manuscript, containing over a thousand species new to science, reached the Netherlands just nine months before Rumphius died. Ironically, the Dutch government deemed the contents of the book to be too valuable and sensitive for publication and embargoed it – only finally allowing it to be published in parts between 1741 and 1755.

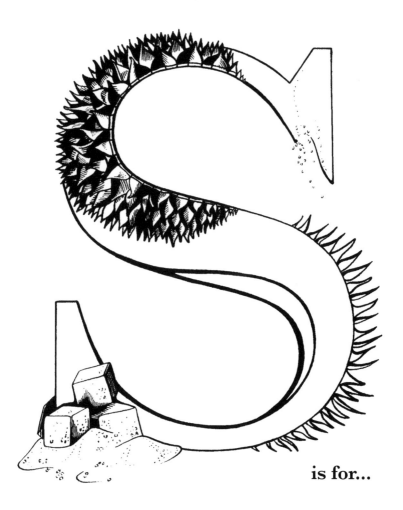

is for...

Saffron

Saffron is said to be the most expensive spice by weight in the world. This comes as no surprise when you learn that it is made from the long crimson stigmas (the female parts of a flower) of *Crocus sativus*, and each crocus produces just three. The golden-red colour of the spice comes from a natural chemical called crocin in the stigmas.

Crocus sativus is thought to be native to the eastern Mediterranean and is a close relative of the crocus bulbs that bloom in our gardens in spring and autumn in the UK. Although relatively easy to grow, around 150 flowers of *Crocus sativus* are needed, each carefully harvested by hand, to produce just one gramme (0.03 ounces) of saffron.

Saffron has long been used medicinally too. Recent research has focused on its potential as an anti-inflammatory and antioxidant. It has been used in a small number of clinical trials to treat depression. Saffron is high in manganese, and Vitamin C and B, and contains anthocyanins (see **E is for Eat your Reds**). Many people espouse the health benefits of drinking saffron tea, but more scientific research is needed.

Scarborough Fair

Are you going to Scarborough Fair? Herbs have been used for medicinal and culinary uses for thousands of years, all over the world. Simon and Garfunkel might not have realised that the combination of parsley, sage, rosemary and thyme that they sang about in their 1968 single was used as a Middle Age version of the contraceptive pill and to induce abortion. 'Going to Scarborough Fair' was a euphemism for the activity that would lead to one getting in the family way in the first place. The optional addition of a black peppercorn was said to increase the effect of the herbs.

We'll leave you to translate this verse of the traditional folk song …

> *Tell him to plough it with a ram's horn,*
> *Parsley, sage, rosemary and thyme;*
> *And sow it all over with one peppercorn,*
> *And he shall be a true lover of mine.*

Sensitive to the Touch

When you're told not to touch something, sometimes you can't help but do so. This is usually the case when you tell people about the sensitive or touch-me-not plant (*Mimosa pudica*). This leguminous species is native to tropical America, but can be found throughout the tropics, often as a weed. It was first described by Carl Linnaeus (see **L, Botany Hero: Carl Linnaeus**) and the species name *pudica* means bashful or shrinking.

The delicate-looking leaves of this pretty plant are famously sensitive to touch (known as seisomonasty), closing quickly in upon themselves as soon as they are touched or stroked. When this property was first investigated by Robert Hooke in the 17th century it was thought that plants had nerves just like animals. Today we know that the leaves fold following a release of chemicals, which causes water to move quickly out of cell vacuoles leading to cell collapse. It is thought that this rapid movement has evolved to deter herbivores of all shapes and sizes.

SMELLIEST FRUIT

Famously banned on several airlines, the Singapore rail network, in many hotels and other public places, the durian is the world's smelliest fruit. Eating one has been described as 'like eating custard in a sewer'. Some say it smells like a dead animal, others compare it to a very ripe blue cheese, but one thing is for certain – it is an acquired taste.

The fruits come from species of *Durio* trees, which grow in the tropical forests of South East Asia. Most of the fruits sold commercially outside of this region come from *Durio zibethinus*. This tree's nectar-rich flowers are pollinated by bats; the flowers then develop into large round spiky fruits up to 3 kg (6.6 lb) in weight.

The distinctive odour becomes apparent when the fruit is ripe. Once the fruit is opened, the aroma can be overwhelming and pervading, hence its ban on public transport. Although the durian enjoys notoriety and a novelty value in the West, it remains a firm favourite in Asia, where it is known as the 'King of Fruits'.

BOTANY HERO
JAMES SOWERBY
(1757–1822)

An extraordinary artist, passionate natural historian, author and teacher, James Sowerby was a whirlwind of productivity. Born to a humble family, fortunately his talent was recognised early on and he was apprenticed to a well-known artist. Soon he was drawing botanical illustrations for one of the foremost botanists and botanical publishers of the day, William Curtis.

Sowerby then went on to hone his skills at the Royal Academy Schools. His talent for accurate and beautiful plant illustrations became much sought after, and it was not long before he was also painting fungi, minerals, fossils and shells for wealthy patrons and publishers.

Sowerby began his own natural history collection and even opened a free museum in his house. As his knowledge and collections grew, he also began to publish his own works, including *Coloured Figures of English Fungi or Mushrooms* (released between 1796 and 1815). This series reveals his great knowledge of fungi, which his biographer Paul Henderson describes as 'a ground-breaking achievement … he became one of principal mycologists in Britain at the time'.

Sowerby published many other important works, including the 36-volume *English Botany*, as well as *Mineral Conchology of Great Britain* and *British Mineralogy*. He described several new species; some such as *Sowerbyella radiculata* (a fungus) were even named after him. His accurate vibrant illustrations, which were indispensable to the scientists of his day, can still give us interesting information today.

SQUIRTING CUCUMBERS

The squirting cucumber (*Ecballium elaterium*) is aptly named.
When the green hairy fruits of this trailing plant are ripe they
explode, squirting their seeds in a torrent of mucilaginous
goo. The seeds can be ejected up to six metres (around 20 ft)
from the parent plant. Although it belongs to the squash
family (Cucurbitaceae), this isn't a cucumber for eating, as all
of its parts are poisonous.

SUGARY SWEETNESS

Most of us consume more sugar than we should. An
increasing number of 'healthier' alternatives to the familiar
white granular sugar are becoming available, but many of
these are no better for us as most are made up of essentially
the same chemical components – simple short-chain
carbohydrates such as sucrose, glucose and fructose.

Most commercially available sugars come from plants.
Plants produce carbohydrates as a result of photosynthesis,
and these in their simplest forms are sugars. Plants store
these sugars in their tissues, to varying degrees, and we then
extract it using a variety of processes.

Sugars are usually found throughout a plant's tissues, but
they may be concentrated in particular storage structures
and tissues, such as in starchy tubers or the central pith of the
plant stem.

Sugar beet (*Beta vulgaris*) forms an underground root
tuber (a bit like a parsnip) from which much of our table
sugar (sucrose) is extracted. Sugar cane (*Saccharum*) is a
genus of tropical grasses, from which sucrose can also be
extracted, and until sugar beet production really took off
in Europe around the time of the Napoleonic Wars, when
shipping was restricted, vast quantities of sugar from sugar

cane were imported from plantations in the West Indies. Sugar cane has such a sweet pith that in the tropics people sometimes cut a stem from a plant when out walking, and chew on it for energy.

Around the world, sugars, and other more complex starchy carbohydrates, are extracted from other plants too, such as the tropical palm species *Arenga pinnata* and *Metroxylon sagu*, as well as several species of *Agave*. Stevia (*Stevia rebaudiana*) is from the daisy family (Asteraceae) and is native to Paraguay, where it has long been used as a sweetener. It is extracted from the leaves of the plant, and is 100–300 times as sweet as sucrose.

SUICIDAL SAGO

Sago is the stuff of many British people's childhood nightmares, with memories of being forced to eat the gelatinous pudding in compulsory school dinners. However, this much-maligned starchy foodstuff is a staple part of the diets of millions of people around the world, particularly in parts of Indonesia such as Papua, New Guinea.

The sago the Papuans eat doesn't look much like British school dinner sago, and is usually either a glue-like paste (eaten after an elaborate twirling of each serving onto the plate), or easily stored and transported dried brick-like cakes that are eaten dry or rehydrated when needed.

Across South East Asia puddings made with pearls of sago are very popular. Elaborate and often colourful sago concoctions have added ingredients like coconut milk, grass jelly cubes, red beans, durian paste, shaved ice and sometimes a handful of Haribo gummy sweets.

Most sago comes from the trunk of the *Metroxylon sagu* palm, but several other palms are sometimes used. It has a so-called 'hapaxanthic' life cycle. Hapaxanthic plants store up all of their energy as they mature, in order to flower in one (often enormous) reproductive effort, after which they die, having used up all of their stored energy. The plant puts all its resources into improving the probability that at least some of its seed will germinate and develop into the next generation.

Such plants are sometimes described as 'suicide' plants as they flower themselves to death. Plants that do not have a hapaxanthic life history are termed 'pleonanthic' and can flower periodically throughout their mature life.

The sago palm is cut down just before flowering starts, before any of the energy stores that the plant has built up as starch in the trunk can be used in the flowering process. The fine white flour is produced by scraping out the starch, grinding, washing and then sieving it.

Did you know? The sago in those old school dinners wasn't sago at all – it was tapioca, a similar-tasting starch made from cassava (*Manihot esculenta*)!

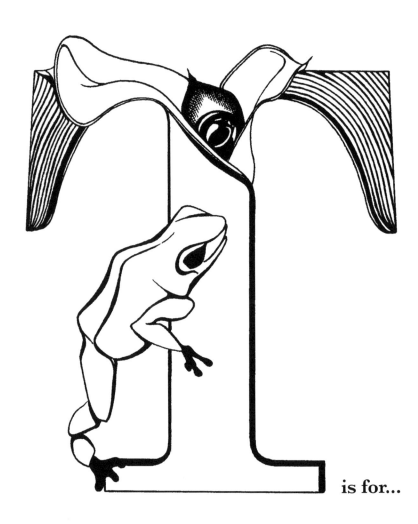

is for...

Tanks up Trees

Bromeliads are a group of weird and wonderful spiky-leaved plants that include the delicious pineapple (see **P is for Pineapple Party Pieces**). Wild species of bromeliads are found almost entirely in the New World. There are 3,000 different species in the family Bromeliaceae, and each is adapted to a different kind of habitat – from arid mountain tops to humid rainforests.

Most bromeliads love warmth and humidity, and some grow high up in the branches of rainforest trees. They have no true roots and are known as epiphytes or 'air plants' (see **H is for High Life**). Some of the most interesting of these are the tank bromeliads, which act as tiny aquaria for a vast range of other species. Some of these species can hold up to 20 litres (over 5 US gallons) of water! Where several of these grow together on a tree branch they can become mini ecosystems where communities of insects including flies, midges and mosquitoes, other invertebrates such as worms, snails and crabs, and animals such as tree frogs, live out their whole lives.

Species of poison-dart frogs (in the genus *Oophaga*) in Central and South America are known to lay their eggs on the forest floor, but once these have hatched into tadpoles the mother carries them up to a chosen bromeliad and drops them into individual pools between the leaves. Here they feed off algae and mosquito larvae, but the mother also returns to lay unfertilised eggs into each pool for them to eat. These eggs supply the tadpoles with the toxins for which the frogs are famous. After 6-8 weeks, tiny poisonous frogs emerge and return to the forest.

Taste of Toona

The leaves of the Chinese toon tree (*Toona sinensis*) taste strongly of onions, and can be picked to use in stir-fries. The young shoots, which are a reddish-brown, are rich in Vitamin A. The wood, bark, fruits and roots of this tree are also useful. The bark is used in Chinese traditional medicine to treat a variety of ailments including flatulence!

Botany Hero
Charlotte Morley Taylor (1955–)

Of the 500 most productive authors of new plant species, just eight have been women. One is still publishing names today – Missouri Botanical Garden's Charlotte Taylor. Taylor is an adjunct professor specialising in neo-tropical Rubiaceae (the coffee family), and has published 278 completely new species to date.

As Charlotte herself says, 'to conserve a plant species, as well as to study its ecology, morphology, human use, secondary chemistry, invasive biology, pests, and other aspects, the species has to be known to science … it needs a clearly identified scientific name. If a species is studied by one researcher, but cannot be re-located by someone else, then any study of it is not testable, because the work can't be repeated – other researchers cannot be sure they are studying the same plants.'

A priority for many botanists around the world remains to describe new species and to publish their names and descriptions so that scientists and conservationists everywhere can know exactly what species they are working on.

Three's Company

Biology students have long been taught about lichens – strange but beautiful organisms made up of two partners – a fungus and either an alga or a cyanobacterium. The fungus creates the protective structure of the lichen while the algae or cyanobacteria are able to provide energy for both organisms via photosynthesis. It is a classic example of 'symbiosis' – more than one organism living together, benefiting each other – the perfect friendship. For 140 years scientists have thought this is how lichens are composed.

New research, led by the University of Montana, has now revealed that another partner is involved – yeasts. Single-celled yeasts have been found in the 'skin' of many lichen species (from 52 different genera, from across the world). Their specific role is now being studied as it may be they provide further structural support or produce other chemicals needed for growth. Much more research is required but, since they have been found in so many different lichen, they are believed to be integral to lichen success. This surprise means that textbooks will have to be re-written, and shows that even research into organisms we think we know well can yield amazing new revelations.

Tiniest Seeds in the World

Contrary to the words of Jesus of Nazareth*, mustard seeds are not the smallest of all seeds on Earth. That honour goes collectively to the seeds of orchid species, of which there are thought to be 30,000 species in the wild.

Orchid seeds are so tiny that they are referred to as 'dust' seed. Many orchid seeds are less than 1 microgramme (ug or mcg) in weight, and typically less than 1 mm (0.04 in) in length. The smallest known seeds are 0.05 mm (0.002 in) in length (*Anoectochilus imitans*), and the largest is 6 mm (*Epidendrum secundum*). Each orchid seed pod can contain huge numbers of these minuscule seeds – a single *Cycnoches chlorochilon* seed pod can contain some 4 million seeds.

Every orchid seed comprises an embryo (which will develop into the new plant) and a seed coat to protect it, but virtually no endosperm – the nutrient-rich food source for the developing, germinating embryo in most plants. Because orchid seeds lack this on-tap food reserve, they cannot easily germinate and start to grow, unless a particular fungal partner is also present in the substrate on which the seed landed – soil, rocks or tree trunks (see **O is for Orchids Take Over the World**).

The fungus provides essential nutrients to the developing orchid embryo, which first becomes a protocorm – a swollen ball of cells that produce chloroplasts and begin to photosynthesize, producing their own energy reserves – and then grows into a seedling. Each orchid species may retain this fungal partner (a mycorrhizal symbiont) for part or all of its life, or may lose its partner completely after germination and grow 'asymbiotically'. It is thought plants of some species may switch between several fungal partners throughout the plant's life.

* According to the Gospel of Mark, chapter 4, verses 30–32: *With what can we compare the Kingdom of God, or what parable will we use for it? It is like a mustard seed, which, when sown upon the ground, is the smallest of all the seeds on Earth.*

TREE LEAVES

Different species of tree have differently shaped leaves, but they also have different quantities of leaves. A mature English oak (*Quercus robur*) has been estimated to have around 700,000 leaves on a single tree, each quietly getting on with the business of photosynthesis (see **C is for Chlorophyll Chemistry**). Meanwhile, it is thought that a single American elm (*Ulmus americana*) may have as many as 5 million leaves!

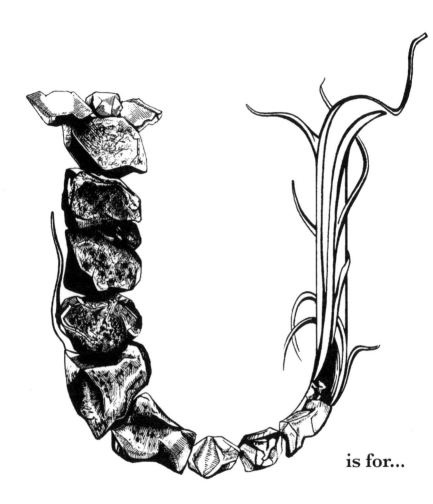

is for...

ULTRAMAFIC

The serpentine soils of places as far flung as the Lizard Peninsula in south-west England, small areas of North America and at least a third of the surface of Grande Terre island in New Caledonia develop from so-called ultramafic rocks.

Rich in nickel, manganese and chromium, these unusual rocks formed in the boundary of the Earth's crust and mantle, deep below the oceans. Plate tectonics resulted in the uplift of such oceanic parts of the crust, and they were forced up and over continental rocks, becoming exposed at the surface – and, much later, were colonised by living organisms.

The unusual composition of ultramafic rocks makes it difficult for most plants to survive on them, especially since they are deficient in nitrogen and phosphorus – critical elements for most plants' healthy growth, as any gardener knows. Plants found on ultramafic soils have therefore evolved to tolerate these difficult conditions and unusual chemistry, by, for instance, accumulating metal ions to reduce their toxicity in critical parts of the plant.

Ultramafic soils therefore have particularly unusual species growing on them, many of which are found nowhere else in the world – including the world's only parasitic conifer, *Parasitaxus usta*, from New Caledonia, and the carnivorous *Darlingtonia californica* from California. Yet with their high concentrations of unusual metals, sites on ultramafic rocks are also often important for the mining of minerals, leading to the increased risk of habitat destruction for these unique plants.

ULTRAVIOLET SIGNPOSTS

We can take great delight in flowers of all sizes, colours and forms, but have you ever stopped to think about how other species view these floral beauties?

Insects, birds and many animals see colours in different ways. Many insects such as bees can see short ultraviolet wavelengths (UV), and some flowers have evolved handy signposts, pointing the way to pollen and nectar by reflecting ultraviolet in a series of patterns and lines known as 'nectar guides'. Flowers are essentially flags to pollinators, and the nectar guides on the petals help them to successfully find the nectar and pollen in a flower.

When you see an image of a flower lit with a UV flash, it's easy to spot these nectar guides because they contrast so strongly with the petals. Some UV markings highlight the entire centre of the flower, like a bull's-eye, while other flowers have runway lights guiding the insects to more concealed nectaries. Some guides are even shaped like arrows.

The anthers, which hold the pollen, can also shine out under UV light. Seen in this way, many common flowers such as pansies, lilies, daisies, iris, hellebores and rock roses look completely different from how we see them, appearing as different colours and revealing a range of hidden cues.

Bees can memorise these markings in order to quickly make choices about which are the best flowers to visit for the most reward, thereby saving vital energy.

UMBRELLA ASSASSINATION

The murder of Georgi Markov (a dissident Bulgarian journalist and author who spoke out about his country's government) on Waterloo Bridge in 1978 at the height of the

Cold War, sounds like a plot from James Bond. Stabbed with the point of an umbrella, embedding a tiny metal pellet in his thigh, Markov died four days later.

The poison the pellet is thought to have contained was ricin, which is 6,000 times more poisonous than cyanide. A dose of ricin weighing the same as a grain of table salt can kill a human. Ricin acts by inactivating the protein-building apparatus in the body's cells, the ribosomes. Without being able to make proteins, normal cellular functioning rapidly breaks down and death slowly but inevitably follows – there is no antidote to ricin's extraordinary potency.

Few people realise that this most deadly toxin comes from the seeds of a plant – and one that is commonly grown as an ornamental in gardens – the castor oil plant (*Ricinus communis*). It is such a tough plant that it is an invasive weed in many places.

Ricinus is related to other members of the spurge family (Euphorbiaceae), including cassava (*Manihot esculenta*), poinsettia (*Euphorbia pulcherrima*) and the Pará rubber tree (*Hevea brasiliensis*) (see **L is for Latex**). Castor oil is extracted from the plant's seeds and used in a wide range of medical, culinary, cosmetic and even engineering commodities (e.g. Castrol used in racing cars). Because ricin is water soluble, it is not extracted with the oil from the seeds, so the oil can be safely consumed. The attractive seeds, sometimes used as beads in necklaces, could mistakenly be eaten by children, and usually pass through the gut without any harm, but if the seeds are chewed or damaged, the ricin in a single seed is enough to kill a child.

UNDERGROUND FORESTS

The 'underground forests' of Africa are an unusual but important component of a type of savannah grassland found mostly in Angola. These grasslands are seasonally burned, and contain a large number of plants known as 'geoxylic suffructices' or 'geoxyles'.

Geoxyles have massive woody below-ground structures, hence being described as 'trees which live underground', forming underground forests. Most closely related to woodland and forest trees, these plants are able to survive the frequent fires in the grasslands, losing their above-ground annual shoots, which regrow from the huge underground organs once the fires have subsided.

Underwater Meadows

You may never have heard of seagrasses, but these unusual marine flowering plants grow in shallow coastal marine habitats, forming vast meadows under the waves. In fact, coastal seagrasses are thought to cover around 200,000 km^2 (over 77,000 square miles) worldwide.

These underwater flowerbeds are home to a wide variety of sea life – including fish, molluscs and crabs, as well as manatees and sea turtles. They help to stabilise the sediments on the sea floor, protecting coastlines from erosion, and help to clean the water. By doing all these things they are fundamental to a healthy marine habitat and also contribute to the livelihoods of millions of people. Perhaps more importantly, they are a very large carbon sink – accounting for an estimated 15 per cent of carbon fixed in the oceans.

There are 72 species of seagrass, which grow around the world; 15 of these species are under threat from extinction due to human activities including pollution and dredging as well as overfishing. The UK's seagrasses – the 'eelgrasses' (*Zostera*), which provide a habitat for rare seahorses – are also sadly in decline. Although they receive little attention, seagrass beds are some of the most productive ecosystems in the world.

Did you know? The widespread eelgrass species *Zostera marina* was the first marine flowering plant to have its genome fully sequenced, early in 2016.

(The Incredible) Uniqueness of Endemism

In the wild, endemic species are found only in one place and nowhere else. Usually a high degree of endemism is likely to be found with a high degree of biodiversity (i.e. total number of species), as is seen in places such as Madagascar where biodiversity levels and species endemism are extremely high. As many as 90 per cent of the approximately 14,000 plant species in Madagascar are only found there (see **M is for Megadiverse Madagascar**).

Knowing about endemism is important for all sorts of reasons and is particularly important – and useful – for conservation. Species endemic to a particular place are often chosen as 'flagship species' for countries, states, organisations, and even local communities, to champion and protect. With limited resources for conservation, prioritising sites and species is essential to determine where funding and time should be focused. Lists of endemic species, and 'percentages of endemism' out of all species found in a site, are important in making such decisions.

As with many important terms, however, 'endemism' can be applied in different ways, and not all endemic species are equivalent. A species endemic to a very specific vegetation type, only found in one geographically small region or country, such as Singapore, may be a higher priority for conservation efforts than a species endemic to a widely distributed, common vegetation type, found across a large region or country such as the USA.

UPSIDE-DOWN TREES

An extraordinary-looking and iconic species, the baobab (*Adansonia digitata*) is known in Africa as the 'upside-down tree'. The disproportionately huge girth of its trunk and its unusual form mean that it is an easy species to spot from afar. It is said that large individuals of this species can store up to 100,000 litres (26,400 US gallons) of water in their trunks. This helps them to endure droughts in the naturally arid landscapes where they grow.

This is an important species for local people – its fruits are rich in Vitamin C and antioxidants, and are either eaten fresh or used to make a drink. The seeds can be used as a thickener for soups, while the leaves are eaten as a vegetable. The fibres from the inner bark are put to use as a string or rope for making baskets and beehives. The roots are used for making dye and various parts of the tree are ingredients in traditional medicines. The baobab is also perceived to have magical properties – a decoction of its seeds is said to protect you from crocodiles.

Did you know? Large individual baobabs are used as meeting places too – some with hollow trunks have been put to use as bus stops or even as pubs. One in Australia was once used as prison.

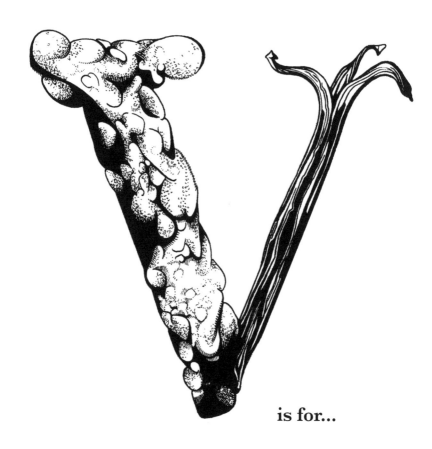

is for...

Valuable Vanilla

Most people are familiar with vanilla as a flavour for ice cream, the little black dots in luxury 'real' custard, or as a sweet slightly floral perfume. What is less known is that vanilla comes from an orchid, in the genus *Vanilla*.

Vanilla is the world's most popular, and arguably the most valuable, spice. It is used in an enormous array of products, often not specifically listed in the ingredients, from those ice creams and custards to yoghurts, salad dressings, chocolate, household cleaning products, fabric softeners, shaving cream, lotions, shampoos, colognes and perfumes. Interestingly, vanilla combines other scents together, softening the edges, and helps such fragrances to last longer on the skin – hence its importance in perfumery.

The vanilla 'bean' is actually an orchid seed pod, the fruit of the plant, with thousands of tiny seeds (see **T is for the Tiniest Seeds**) – those little black dots in the custard – each theoretically able to grow into a new plant.

Although there are approximately 100 species in the genus, only a few *Vanilla* species are used commercially. The most common of those, *Vanilla planifolia*, is originally from the forests of Mexico, where it is pollinated by a specific bee species. In the vanilla plantations of Madagascar, Indonesia and other parts of the world, the pollinating bee is not found, so each flower has to be hand-pollinated – and each flower is only open for eight hours, opening in the early morning and closing by midday.

The time-consuming pollination cannot be automated, nor can farmers control when the flowers open on different plants. Nine months' development of each pod follows before they can be harvested, again by hand. The pods are then cured and processed to develop their fragrance and flavours, taking several more months.

From young plant through to a fine-grade vanilla bean takes a long, labour-intensive, skilful set of stages until the pods are ready for sale and export – which helps to explain why each vanilla pod is so expensive to buy.

Vegetable Propaganda

Carrots are undoubtedly good for you – packed with Vitamins K and B6, as well as Vitamin A (beta-carotene). In the UK we eat, on average, around 100 carrots per person, every year. What they can't do for you, unfortunately, is help you to see in the dark. So where did this old wives' tale come from? Answer: The Royal Air Force.

In the Second World War, the RAF needed an excuse as to why their pilots were suddenly able to have greater success in their night raids and battles. They were desperate to keep their advances in radar technology secret. Eating carrots became the official explanation from the government, and the myth that they could help you to see in the dark was born. This also had the benefit of encouraging everyone to eat more home-grown veg. So, next time you eat a carrot make sure you thank it for helping defeat tyranny.

Did you know? Carrots have not always been orange: their wild ancestor (*Daucus carota*) actually produces spindly tough little taproots that are purple in colour. Cultivation began around 1,000 years ago in Persia (Afghanistan, Pakistan and Iran today) and a yellow variant is thought to be the source of the larger, sweeter cultivars that have emerged today. Purple carrots are still grown in Afghanistan, and purple varieties are becoming increasingly available in the UK, adding interest and colour to our dinner plates.

VEGETABLE SHEEP

Yes, these are real and no, they're not sheep. The name 'vegetable sheep' actually refers to two very striking genera of alpine plants – *Haastia* and *Raoulia*. Both are endemic to New Zealand. These woolly-leaved hummock-forming plants are so named because they do indeed resemble sheep from a distance, making them true botanical oddities.

Both genera are in the daisy family (Asteraceae), and the term 'vegetable sheep' is mainly applied to *Raoulia eximia* and *R. mammillaris,* both of which are very compact, rounded cushion plants. Some individuals can reach up to two metres across!

The leaves of *Raoulia* are actually a bluish-green, but they are densely covered with white hairs, giving them their woolly appearance. The leaves are packed together in rosettes in a dense mass, so that only the tips are visible. This is an adaptation to the harsh mountain environment in which these plants live – protecting the leaves from cold winds and harsh sunlight. Close up, *Raoulia eximia* is a particularly beautiful plant, its rosettes of leaves form geometric patterns, while its crimson flowers are a mere 3 mm (0.125 in) across.

VOLATILE OILS

Flowers release some beautiful scents (made of organic molecules that evaporate into the air) in order to attract pollinators, but did you know that many plants also release volatile oils from their leaves, buds and other parts? These have a variety of effects – from suppressing pest attacks and inhibiting bacteria to reducing competition from other plants. Some plant groups are particularly known for their volatile oil content including conifers, citrus and plants in the myrtle, carrot and mint families (Myrtaceae, Apiaceae and Lamiaceae, respectively).

Familiar Mediterranean herbs such as rosemary, oregano and thyme, as well as spices including cinnamon and clove, generate volatile (or 'essential') oils, and it is these that give their leaves aromatic qualities and flavour. They have also been shown to have antimicrobial and antifungal properties.

Pine trees release volatile oils when they're attacked by pine aphids. The oils fill the air and carry on the breeze. This then attracts aphid predators such as ladybirds, who follow the scent trail to the trees where their unsuspecting prey are waiting.

Forests of *Eucalyptus* trees can release such a quantity of volatile oil that they appear to be surrounded by a blue haze. In fact, this is how the Blue Mountains near Sydney in Australia got their name. The oils can also leach out of fallen *Eucalyptus* leaves into the soil, suppressing other vegetation from growing around the trees.

However, the oils are also highly flammable – Australian and Mediterranean habitats are notoriously subject to wildfires above a certain temperature threshold. Species adapted to these environments often have seeds that are fire- or heat-resistant and stimulated into growth by smoke.

For us, plant volatile oils may have great potential in a variety of ways – from preventing food spoilage to repelling insects such as mosquitoes, and deterring pests from valuable crops.

Vortex Rings

Sphagnum mosses are extraordinary plants. They may appear quite primitive – and indeed mosses were one of the earliest land plants to evolve – but they are still sophisticated and successful organisms. There are around 285 species of *Sphagnum*, and these are thought to cover about one per cent of the world's land surface. But they do have limitations – their height being one.

If you're low to the ground, how do you get your spores up into the air and away on the breeze to help create the next generation? *Sphagnum* spore capsules have walls that dry out, making their walls shrink until they pop open in an explosive way, jettisoning the spores at a speed of around 80 km (50 miles) per hour. But, they also have a neat trick to make them go further – they use the power of a vortex ring.

The exploding capsule propels the spores upwards in a miniature mushroom cloud that allows them to move further up into the air column – up to a height of around 11–16 cm (4–6 in), where they can catch the breeze and move out to establish new plants further away.

This discovery in 2010, by American scientists Dwight Whitaker and Joan Edwards, was the first time vortex rings had been seen to be used by a plant.

is for...

Walking Palms

Everyone knows that plants don't walk, don't they? Except the so-called 'walking palm', *Socratea exorrhiza*, from Central and South America ... sort of. The story of the walking palm, moving around the forest from shade to sunlight, is a much-repeated part of forest guides' tales to tourists; they swear blind to any visitor that no *Socratea* palm is where it was last time they followed a particular trail.

The name *exorrhiza* refers to the stilt roots (rhiza) of the species, which grow above the ground and upon which the main trunk of the palm stands – giving the impression that the palm has many legs. Really, each 'leg' is a root connecting the trunk to the ground.

The theory, first presented in 1980 by John H. Bodley, is that the palm is able to actively grow new roots in one direction, and the old roots on the other side slowly lift into the air and die away. Bodley proposed that this mechanism would allow the palm to move away from hazards, such as a tree falling nearby, and some researchers estimated that the palms could move up to 2–3 cm (1 inch) per day in response to stimuli.

Unfortunately, as appealing as the theory might have been, it was never scientifically proven. In 2005, Costa Rican biologist Gerardo Avalos published an in-depth study of *Socratea*, debunking the theory by showing that the roots do not move and, although the roots may die off periodically, the trunk remains in one place over time.

Botany Hero
Alfred Russel Wallace (1823–1913)

Today's most famous natural historian Sir David Attenborough said of Alfred Russel Wallace 'there is no more admirable character in the history of science'. High praise indeed and rightly deserved. Wallace is famous (although not famous enough) for several things – first and foremost of which is his contribution to the theory of evolution by natural selection. He deduced this theory while in the wilds of South East Asia and wrote to Charles Darwin about it from the island of Ternate. They published the theory together in 1858 and changed biological science forever (See **D, Botany Hero: Charles Darwin**).

His other great theoretical discovery is now known as Wallace's Line – a conceptual biological boundary that separates Australasia and Asia and coincides with the tectonic plates below these landmasses and their seas. The plants and animals found on either side of this invisible boundary running through the Lombok Strait and east of Borneo and the Philippines are quite distinctly different from each other. The particular plants and animals found on one side of the line are not found on the other, and vice versa, even though a relatively narrow stretch of water separates the land masses. The research that led to Wallace proposing this boundary (in 1859) has also led to him becoming known as the 'Father of Evolutionary Biogeography'. The area of Indonesian islands to the east of the Wallace Line is also known as Wallacea.

Wallace's enormous legacy of significant achievements across several disciplines is often overshadowed by the celebration of Darwin's work, but in his day he was just as famous, and now should be again.

Did you know? A new genus of palm was named after Wallace by botanists at the Royal Botanic

Gardens, Kew to mark the 100th anniversary of
Wallace's death in 2013. The single species in this
genus, *Wallaceodoxa raja-ampat*, was described from
specimens on the islands of Raja Ampat to the west of
New Guinea. Wallace visited these islands in 1860 as he
travelled through the region.

WITCHES AND WARLOCKS

There was a time, not so very long ago, when you wouldn't
want to leave home without a bit of mandrake in your pocket,
especially if you thought you were at risk from witchcraft.
Many plants came by their Latin and common names because
they were associated with the protection of saints or angels or
were good at repelling evil spirits.

St John's wort (*Hypericum perforatum*) is a beautiful yellow-
flowered plant that flowers around St John's Day (24 June),
and has a long history of being used to ward off the devil.
Plants thought to have these protective powers were hung
in homes, over thresholds or in communal places, and were
worn by individuals. Wormwood (*Artemisia*) was said to
protect you against flying evil things (and fittingly it is used
in some anti-malarial drugs today), while carrying mandrake
root or wearing a marigold also drove away witches.

Other plants were used in helping to 'detect' witches.
Some sources claim that bouquets of marjoram, rue, broom,
agrimony and other plants were presented to suspects, who
if they could not abide the smell were then revealed as being
in league with the devil. And should you fall prey to a witch,
plants such as scarlet pimpernel and rowan were said to be
effective in counteracting certain spells.

Botany Hero
Ernest Henry 'Chinese' Wilson
(1876–1930)

There are few gardens today that don't contain at least one plant introduced by Ernest Henry Wilson. Wilson is one of history's greatest plant hunters, responsible for over a thousand new species being brought into cultivation.

Wilson was extremely canny at knowing which plants were the most garden-worthy. From stunning herbaceous plants through a wide variety of flowering shrubs to many delightful tree species, including birch, maple and cherries, he collected an astonishing variety of plants from the wilds of central and western China. Many of his introductions proved to be species new to science.

Originally a gardener at the Birmingham Botanical Gardens and at the Royal Botanic Gardens, Kew, Wilson then studied botany, and was soon recommended by the director of Kew as a plant collector for the famous Veitch nurseries. He went on to complete four plant-hunting expeditions to China between 1899 and 1911, and developed a fascination with the country, its flora and its people – so much so that he earned the nickname 'Chinese' Wilson.

Wilson not only collected live plants and seeds but also made over 18,000 herbarium specimens and took many thousands of photographs, both of which are proving to be invaluable today. His adventures have filled several books, but his legacy is to be found in the superb plants that he brought to the West – including the handkerchief tree (*Davidia involucrata*), the Chinese dogwood (*Cornus kousa*), Wilson's magnolia (*Magnolia wilsonii*), the regal lily (*Lilium regale*), the poppies *Meconopsis integrifolia* and *M. punicea*, as well as species of *Rhododendron, Sorbus, Acer, Viburnum, Primula, Clematis, Iris* and *Rosa,* among many others. Wilson's skills changed the face of gardens across Europe and America.

WONDERFUL WOLLEMI

In 1994, the botanical world was in a state of high excitement when a 'living fossil' was discovered in a remote gorge of the Wollemi National Park in the Blue Mountains of Australia. A park ranger called David Noble had come across a stand of 40 tall trees with unusual leaves and brown 'coco-pop' bark, and knew he had never seen this species before.

After some deliberation, botanists agreed that this was in fact a new species, related to the monkey puzzle tree (*Araucaria araucana*) and belonging to a genus thought to have gone extinct 65 million years ago. It was duly named *Wollemia nobilis.*

Because so few trees were found, a large-scale propagation plan was put in place to ensure the survival of the species. Specimens were sent to the Royal Botanic Gardens, Kew, and elsewhere, to test their hardiness in the northern hemisphere, and were so at home in the UK that it was not long before Wollemi pines were propagated for sale and marketed as 'dinosaur trees'.

The sale of the saplings has helped to fund the conservation of their native habitat and preserve the species. A true 'rags to riches' story – this species has gone from being presumed extinct to one that is widely available in garden centres today.

Did you know? The oldest Wollemi pine is thought to be over 1,000 years old and is known affectionately as King Billy. With so few wild specimens, this species is classified by the IUCN as Critically Endangered (see **R is for Red Alert!**).

WORM-EATERS

Nearly all us have heard of Venus fly traps (*Dionaea muscipula*), which like to snap their traps shut on unsuspecting insects, but there are plenty of other bizarre ways in which plants have evolved to feed on animals – from the liquid-filled traps of pitcher plants such as *Nepenthes* and *Sarracenia*, to the sticky flytrap leaves of sundews (*Drosera*) and butterworts (*Pinguicula*).

One plant you that probably won't have heard of is *Philcoxia* from Brazil. There are three species in the genus, all of which live in nutrient-poor white sand. They have evolved to trap and feed on nematode worms. Each plant has an array of up to one hundred tiny (around 1mm across) sticky leaves that lie just under the surface of the sand. The leaves have stalked glands, which ooze sticky secretions, while protein-digesting enzymes take care of any unwary worm that is unfortunate enough to get stuck. *Philcoxia* are the only plants with sticky leaves known to feed on worms, and the only plants known to use underground leaves as traps.

is for...

X-Rated Plants

Many plants have been given the label of 'aphrodisiac' over the years (sometimes without much evidence of their effects). Some are quite surprising and are now common ingredients in much of our cuisine – including parsley, onion, fennel, saffron and nutmeg. Others, including chocolate and coffee, are perhaps more obvious. However, one plant from Peru has a folklore dating back centuries as to its libidinous qualities.

Maca (*Lepidium meyenii*) comes from the high cold mountains of the Central Andes in Peru, where it has been cultivated for thousands of years both as an energising food and as a presumed fertility aid. A member of the cabbage family (Brassicaceae), this species is also known as 'Peruvian Viagra' and has long been used by local people to increase sexual desire, virility, stamina and performance.

Scientists have recently begun to look at maca as an aid to sexual dysfunction and fertility problems in wider society. Maca contains some important secondary metabolites including those known as macamides, which are thought to act upon hormone levels. Consumption of maca has increased significantly in recent years, but while some proof exists as to its effectiveness much further research is required into all of its effects as well as its safety.

Xerophytes

Lots of plants around the world have evolved to endure extraordinarily harsh conditions; conditions in which human beings could not survive for long. Some of the toughest plants are found in hot, dry deserts, and on the tops of cold, windswept mountains. The crucial similarity between these two extreme habitats is the absence of liquid water found in both – so-called 'xeric' conditions. Plants which have evolved adaptations to survive xeric conditions are called 'xerophytes'.

Adaptations may involve the ability to store water inside fleshy, succulent tissues with thick epidermal layers to reduce transpiration of water, and plants often have defences such as spines to deter herbivory by thirsty animals, as seen in species of *Aloe* in Africa and the Middle East, and cacti in the Americas. Bromeliads (see **T is for Tanks up Trees**) are often drenched in tropical forests, but are also exposed to periods without any water at all, and have xerophytic adaptations such as small scale-like cells that stop water evaporating from the plant. Other plants may store water in swollen organs buried deep underground, or they may form small mound- or rosette-shaped plants low to the ground to reduce their exposure to the drying air (see also **G is for Geophytic Ground-Huggers**).

Eagle-eyed filmgoers may have spotted a few small, but unmistakably botanical, hummock-shapes of xerophytic plants in some scenes in *The Martian*, which was shot in desert locations in Jordan. Plants get everywhere. Even in the remotest, most extreme environments on Earth, you can almost always find plants. Not on the real Mars though.

eXtremely Tiny Flowering Plants

If you've got a pond in your garden you may be familiar with duckweed – covering the surface of the water with tiny specks of green, providing handy camouflage for frogs. It's an easy plant to take for granted, but the duckweeds are quite remarkable for they include the smallest flowering plant in the world. There are several genera of tiny plants in this group, but *Wolffia* species are the smallest, with leaves often less than a millimetre long.

Each floating, rootless plant has two small oval leaves and produces a single flower that is so small you need a microscope to see it. The flowers consist of a stigma and a single stamen. The resulting fruits often measure between 0.25 mm and 0.4 mm (0.01–0.15 inch) across. Two of the smallest species are *W. angusta* from Australia and *W. globosa* from Asia and Africa.

This genus of plants is often also called 'watermeal' and has been used as a good source of protein in Asia. Despite their tiny size, duckweeds can take over entire lakes and rivers if not managed properly as they are highly effective at reproducing vegetatively.

XYLOSMA

There are definite pitfalls to being unique, especially when you only grow in a certain place on a single volcanic island. When the volcano on the island of Montserrat, in the eastern Caribbean, erupted between 1995 and 1997 it sent pyroclastic flows (an explosive outflow of superheated gas and rock) over large parts of the island, destroying the capital city and several villages.

Three species of plant are endemic to Montserrat – meaning they grow nowhere else. These are the stunning Montserrat orchid (*Epidendrum montserratense*), an unusual species from the coffee family known as pribby (*Rondeletia buxifolia*) and a member of the willow family called *Xylosma serrata*.

Scientists and horticulturists from the Royal Botanic Gardens, Kew, worked closely with local partners in Monserrat to help save plant species under threat from the after-effects of the eruption and plan for their conservation.

In 2006, Kew went to the island to mount a search for *Xylosma serrata*. Historically, this species had only been seen in one valley in the Soufrière Hills, and that was now under the largest of the pyroclastic deposits. Despite several searches for this plant, it has not been found to date, leading it to be declared 'Critically Endangered, Possibly Extinct' by the IUCN.

Thankfully, the Monserrat orchid and the pribby fared much better and healthy populations of both these precious species now exist.

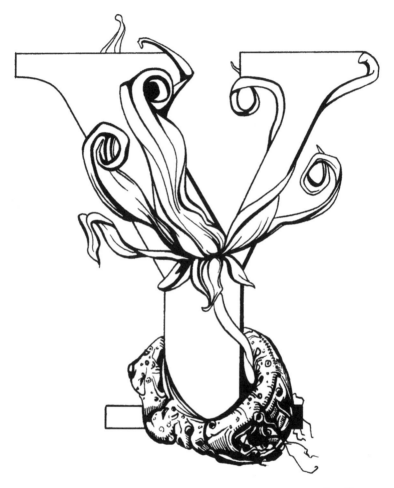

is for...

Yams Like Elephant's Feet

Yams are the tubers of plants in the genus *Dioscorea*, of which there are over 600 known species, found in all tropical and subtropical regions of the world. Many of these tubers are edible, and they form important components of diets in many countries, including rural parts of Madagascar. Work is taking place there to introduce more sustainable ways of cultivation to alleviate the need for people to collect threatened species of yams from the wild.

Probably the most bizarre yam species is *Dioscorea elephantipes*, from South Africa, also known as the elephant's foot yam. The plant has shrubby stems that twine towards the ends, and an enormous swollen tuber, which is mostly found above ground. The greyish tuber, which gives the plant its common name, is pear-shaped and has a cracked surface, with thick cork-like plates. Unfortunately, this slow-growing species suffers from over-collection for horticulture and medicinal uses in its native South Africa, and it is likely to be threatened with extinction.

Did you know? Sweet potatoes (*Ipomoea batatas*) are sometimes called yams, especially in the USA, but they are completely unrelated to real yams, and are members of the morning glory family (Convolvulaceae).

Yawn-Inducing Lettuces

As the base ingredient of most salads, you would think that the benign lettuce would have no negative effect on you whatsoever. However, some wild species of lettuce, including *Lactuca virosa*, have a certain reputation, as every Beatrix Potter fan knows. The opening line of *The Tale of The Flopsy Bunnies* reads: 'It is said that the effect of eating too much lettuce is "soporific"'. It appears alongside a sweet illustration of six baby rabbits fast asleep under a lettuce plant in Mr McGregor's garden. Miss Potter may have possibly based this on her copy of the 16th-century Gerard's *Herball*, but also on contemporary science.

Several wild species of *Lactuca* exude a milky fluid, called lactucarium, when their leaves are cut – this is known by some as 'lettuce opium' and can act as a sedative. Lactucarium contains active chemical compounds, including lactucin, and was once commonly used in cough medicines and in sedatives and analgesics. If eaten in sufficient quantities, wild lettuces can, reportedly, have toxic effects – another fact known to owners of pet rabbits.

However, before you start stocking your drugs cabinet with lettuce, it's worth remembering that modern cultivated lettuces (of *Lactuca sativa*) have had the bitterness bred out of them, and along with it much of their sedative quality.

(Useful) Yews

Paclitaxel (brand name Taxol) is an important treatment for ovarian and breast cancer, and other solid tumours, and originates from that instantly recognisable tree of English churchyards, the yew. Originally paclitaxel was isolated from the bark of *Taxus brevifolia*, the Pacific yew, in the 1960s by US researchers who screened hundreds of plants for potentially useful medicinal properties. However, the process of removing the bark from the slow-growing trees kills the plant, and harvesting it is not sustainable.

It was quickly realised that it was not possible to harvest enough bark to meet demand for the drug. Researchers looked at relatives of the Pacific yew, other species in the genus *Taxus*, to see if they could find the same or similarly active compounds. By the early 1990s methods had been devised to use the leaf clippings of the European yew, *Taxus baccata*, to extract a precursor chemical that could then be processed in the lab to produce paclitaxel.

Using the leaf clippings of yews is a much less destructive and therefore more sustainable way to ultimately produce the drug than stripping the bark. Now methods have been developed to use cultured plant cells on an industrial scale to produce paclitaxel, removing the need to harvest even the yew needles.

Did you know? People have been using yews for many centuries – for tools, weapons, musical instruments and in religion and folklore, especially in pagan traditions. In churchyards, yews are symbols of resurrection, and some of these yews are among Britain's oldest trees.

YLANG-YLANG

A perfume so beautiful they named it twice, ylang-ylang is most familiar to us as an essential oil and as an ingredient in high-end perfumes such as Chanel No. 5. This sweet floral scent actually comes from the flowers of *Cananga odorata* – a tree native to a broad region known as the tropical Indo-Pacific. This species has long been revered and indeed cultivated for its perfumed flowers.

Sir Joseph Banks, the naturalist who travelled with Captain Cook on HMS *Endeavour*, wrote about ylang-ylang in his journal. He described this member of the custard-apple family (Annonaceae) as having a scent that was 'agreeable, but altogether peculiar to itself'. Obviously he wasn't much of a perfume lover.

The unusual flowers of ylang-ylang consist of six long, narrow, drooping yellow-green petals that often curl slightly at the ends. These are picked and then steam-distilled to obtain the essential oil for making perfume. Around 100 tonnes (110 US tons) of this floral oil are produced every year.

An inferior product called cananga oil is also produced from ylang-ylang trees. Most oil is commercially distilled today in Madagascar and Indonesia.

Did you know? The common name is thought to have come from a word in some Philippine languages that means 'something that flutters'.

is for...

Zero Gravity

News reports in 2016 of the first plant to flower in space, an orange *Zinnia* on board the International Space Station, were surprisingly behind the times.

The Soviet Union was the first to successfully flower an extraterrestrial plant, the unassuming cruciferous species *Arabidopsis thaliana* (thale cress), back in 1982 on board the Salyut-7 space station. This tiny flowering plant has long been used as a 'model' by research scientists seeking to understand plant genetics, biochemical pathways and development.

Its 40-day life cycle, from seed germination through to seed production, made *Arabidopsis* the perfect plant to take on early space missions to investigate the effect of the zero (or rather, micro) gravity and radiation levels experienced in low Earth orbit. Since then, a range of plants have been grown (and sometimes flowered) in space, including romaine lettuce, courgette, sunflowers, broccoli, wheat and *Brassica rapa*. Producing fresh food will be an important part of future long-term space missions and manned missions to Mars and beyond.

Zingy Zingibers

Traditionally, ginger biscuits are eaten to combat nausea, for example from travel sickness or morning sickness, and lemon and ginger tea is taken to treat sore throats and colds. Ginger (*Zingiber officinale*) is a well-known medicinal root – more accurately known as a rhizome (an underground stem) – and is closely related to turmeric (*Curcuma longa*) and cardamom (*Elettaria cardamomum*). These three economically-important species are cultivated and traded internationally.

The ginger family (Zingiberaceae) comprises approximately 1,200 species, which grow in tropical forests worldwide. Most species are found in Asia, between India and New Guinea. The fleshy fruits of some species of gingers are eaten by humans and animals, the leafy shoots are sometimes eaten by animals, while the rhizomes are used for medicinal and culinary purposes, and the seeds as spices.

Another important spice belonging to the ginger family is grains of paradise (*Aframomum melegueta*), originally from Western Africa. It is a peppery, citrusy spice now used to flavour several brands of gin. *Le Ménagier de Paris*, a medieval book of instruction dating from 1393, advised that the grains, then often a substitute for more expensive black pepper, could be used to refresh old, stale wine.

Zombies

There are some plants that contain compounds with the power to alter our perceptions and mood, and even our state of consciousness. Many of these 'psychoactive' plants have been used in traditional rituals and ceremonies down the ages, and some continue to be used in this way today (see **H is for Hallucinogenic**). Such rituals often took place to help shamans or leaders contact the 'spirit world' for guidance. However, several of these plants have been used for an altogether darker purpose.

Brugmansia and *Datura* are two closely related South American genera of plants in the nightshade family (Solanaceae), which are commonly known as angels' trumpets. Although they can be useful medicinally in carefully prepared low doses (for external applications), parts of these plants have profound and dangerous effects when ingested. The fruits of *Datura stramonium* (thorn apple) and *D. metel* have been called zombie cucumbers in Haiti, and have reportedly been used to induce a state of near-death.

Brugmansia contain the active tropane alkaloids scopolamine and atropine, as well as over 20 other alkaloids. These block signals between nerve endings and can stop the central nervous system from working properly. Depending on the dose, this can result in anything from slurred speech to hallucinations and even a coma.

Historically, the paralysis and coma caused by these plants was taken advantage of during the ceremonial rites surrounding the burial of elite men in parts of Colombia, where the slaves and wives of the deceased had to accompany him to his grave. These people were given powdered *Brugmansia* mixed with a maize beer (*chicha*) and tobacco leaves, which effectively turned them into zombies, and they were then buried alive with their dead master.

ZOOPHILOUS

Many plants have evolved weird and wonderful mechanisms to attract animals, and as such are hugely important components in the web of life. When plants have adapted to be pollinated by birds, reptiles, bats and other mammals they are referred to as zoophilous.

Flower colour plays an important part – bright red showy flowers are attractive to birds, especially hummingbirds, honeyeaters and sunbirds, while pale scented flowers, which are more noticeable at night, are a big draw for bats. Around a third of bat species have been observed visiting flowers at night.

Some flowers have become highly adapted to these nocturnal visitors, such as the jade vine (*Strongylodon macrobotrys*) from the Philippines (see **J is for Jade Vine**). This species has large pendulous sprays of pale jade-green flowers, which the bats access by hanging upside down on the inflorescence.

Mammals are thought to be important pollinators of flowers at night. Rodent pollination is rare, although a nocturnal short-snouted elephant shrew and striped field mice are known to pollinate the scented blooms of the small parasitic plant *Cytinus visseri* (the northern vampire cup) in South Africa. Mice, gerbils and possums have also been recorded visiting plants and pollinating them in South Africa and Australia.

Nectar-loving lizards, including geckos and skinks, are other important pollinators, being particularly drawn to highly-scented flowers. This is especially important on islands where other pollinators might be limited. One of the first examples of lizard pollination was recorded on Madeira, but other examples are known from New Zealand, Tasmania, Mauritius, Madagascar and elsewhere.

These animals are all attracted by nectar, so plants that rely on vertebrates produce copious amounts of it to ensure their visitor stays long enough to get covered in pollen to carry to the next flower, thus completing the process of pollination. The resulting fruits are also a huge draw for animals, who return to feast upon them and then disperse the seeds along with some useful fertilizer for the new seedlings.

Recommended Reading for More Amazing Facts and Stories About the Plant Kingdom

A is for Arsenic: The Poisons of Agatha Christie, **Kathryn Harkup**

Bizarre Plants: Magical, Monstrous, Mythical, **William A. Emboden**

Curry: A Tale of Cooks and Conquerors, **Lizzie Collingham**

Gin Glorious Gin, **Olivia Williams**

Ginkgo: The Tree that Time Forgot, **Peter Crane**

Imperial Nature: Joseph Hooker and the Practices of Victorian Science, **Jim Endersby**

Indulgence: One Man's Search for the Best Chocolate, **Paul Richardson**

James Sowerby: The Enlightenment's Natural Historian, **Paul Henderson**

Kew magazine, **Royal Botanic Gardens, Kew**

Kingdom of Plants: A Journey through their Evolution, **Will Benson**

Marianne North: A Very Intrepid Painter, **Michelle Payne**

Monkey Puzzle Man: Archibald Menzies, Plant Hunter, **James McCarthy**

Natural Histories: 25 Extraordinary Species that have Changed our World, **Brett Westwood and Stephen Moss**

Pharaoh's Flowers: The Botanical Treasures of Tutankhamun, **Nigel Hepper**

Plants: from Roots to Riches, **Kathy Willis and Carolyn Fry**

The Big, Bad Book of Botany: The World's Most Fascinating Flora, **Michael Largo**

The Botanical Treasury: Celebrating 40 of the World's Most Fascinating Plants through Historical Art and Manuscripts, **curated by Christopher Mills**

The Cabaret of Plants: Botany and the Imagination, **Richard Mabey**

The Invention of Nature: The Adventures of Alexander von Humboldt, the Lost Hero of Science, **Andrea Wulf**

The Last Great Plant Hunt: The Story of Kew's Millennium Seed Bank, **Carolyn Fry, Sue Seddon and Gail Vines**

The Plant Hunters: The Adventures of the World's Greatest Botanical Explorers, **Carolyn Fry**

The Strangest Plants in the World, **S. Talalaj and D. & J. Talalaj**

The World of Kew (A New Year at Kew), **Carolyn Fry**

Vanilla Orchids: Natural History and Cultivation, **Ken Cameron**

Wicked Plants: The A–Z of Plants that Kill, Maim, Intoxicate and Otherwise Offend, **Amy Stewart**

Index of common names

INDEX OF SCIENTIFIC NAMES